CW00429660

ADVANCE TO VICTORY

Battleground Europe
ADVANCE TO VICTORY

Michael Stedman

Series editor
Nigel Cave

LEO COOPER

First published in 2001 by
LEO COOPER
an imprint of
Pen & Sword Books Limited
47 Church Street, Barnsley, South Yorkshire S70 2AS

Copyright © Michael Stedman, 2001

ISBN 0 85052 670 1

A CIP catalogue of this book is available
from the British Library

Printed by CPI UK

*For up-to-date information on other titles produced under the Leo Cooper imprint,
please telephone or write to:*
Pen & Sword Books Ltd, FREEPOST, 47 Church Street
Barnsley, South Yorkshire S70 2AS
Telephone 01226 734222

CONTENTS

Introduction by Series Editor

Until now the *Battleground Europe* series has concentrated, on the Somme battlefield, upon the events of 1916. This has been for a multitude of reasons: the first time that many of the Kitchener men saw major action on the front, and for all too many their last time; because the area covered in any one part of the battle was so relatively small; perhaps, above all, because that is where much of the interest of the visitor lies. Far less well known are the events around the Hindenburg Line and Arras, the German spring and summer offensives of 1918 and least known of all, the British offensive of the late summer and autumn of 1918.

There seems to be something quite contrary about the British character which likes to dwell upon failure or relative failure. Even the tremendous triumph of 1918 has, to a considerable extent, been hijacked in popular perception by the Australians and Canadians. This is not to say that the achievements of these Dominions were not considerable, even outstanding. But they have been allowed to overshadow all that the Imperial troops achieved elsewhere on the front, notably here on the Somme. Some of this may be explained, as Dr Steve Badsey has recently pointed out, by the fact that censorship rules allowed Corps to be identified in the press – thus ANZAC and the Canadian Corps often found themselves in the news column. On the other hand, I Corps or XIV Corps does not have the same ring, and in any case the divisions in any Corps changed considerably according to circumstances.

This book will help to set right the balance, concentrating as it does on the events north of the Somme, which were to whisk the British army over the old Somme battlefields in a matter of weeks (for the attack over the Ancre, heading south eastwards, in a matter of days) and was to reach its culmination with the triumphant breaching of the Hindenburg Line by the end of September.

All of this was achieved with divisions that had been sorely tried during the German onslaught earlier in the year. Some division's, like the 21st, had already had well over 12,000 casualties by the time that it emerged from the last of three major battles, down on the Aisne sector, in June 1918. It then lost rather more casualties in the subsequent Advance to Victory, fighting battle after battle from mid August 1918 until the armistice. It really was an extraordinary achievement, notable, as Mike Stedman points out, for the significant number of eighteen-year olds who formed such a large part of this force.

The reader (and traveller) will be taken over much of the ground which they will find familiar from their studies of the 1916 battlefield. But now they will have to look at it with new eyes and appreciate it in the context of new circumstances, technological and military. The battles of 1918 deserve to be as well known as those of 1916; the actions of generals, so denigrated in 1916, need to be studied and appreciated; the huge numbers of men who died or suffered in 1918 have the same right to be remembered as those who fell in 1916. Lest we Forget.

Nigel Cave
St Mary's, Derryswood

Author's Introduction

The Somme is often walked by visitors who are intent upon the tragic and static events of 1915 and 1916. My purpose within this book is to help redress that balance and to demonstrate the remarkable part played in the final defeat of Germany by the British Army in August 1918 at the outset of the final one hundred days. To the south of the River Somme the Australian and Canadian divisions' successes at the Battle of Amiens are legendary, but here, around the old 1916 battlefield and south to the River Somme itself, the genuinely British element of the Allied effort is an incredible story in its own right - and one well suited to the form of this guidebook. This is a story which has mobility and the hope of a foreseeable end to more than four years of barren and ugly warfare. For the 18 and 19 year olds who formed a significant part, in many cases the greater part, of many British infantry units in the last weeks of the war the outcome is testimony to those young men's resilience and to the organisational qualities which enabled the army to mould those untried soldiers into units capable of playing a major role in the winning of the war. In this respect the debate about whether or not Haig was simply fortunate to be sat on the right horse at the war's end or whether he was indeed the man responsible for organising and motivating the British Army's final and finest contribution to the defeat of Germany will rage on. But this book is not intended to add to that debate.

Within the chronology and narrative of this complex story I have often referred to unit histories at a divisional level. These reveal that the casualties incurred among units which fought during the August to September period across the Somme battlefield were often heavy and only exceeded by those recorded in the terrible summer of 1916 and the autumn of 1917 below Passchendaele. For the ordinary infantryman late 1918 was therefore a dangerous period in the Great War's story.

I am fortunate in not having been to war and am therefore doubly privileged to be involved in the process of making this sort of history accessible. My only motivation is to bring people to these places with a willingness to learn and find out what happened. This guide is not an attempt to tell all there is to know - but rather its purpose is to open the window which will enable you to seek understanding. Whether you are the family of a soldier and combatant, a student or teacher trying to make the most of an organised visit, a casual visitor or an enthusiast, young or old alike, this is a most remarkable classroom - the Somme Battlefield.

Michael Stedman.
Leigh, Worcester.

Acknowledgements

It would have been impossible to complete this guide without the help of many of my contemporaries. In particular I should like to thank Nigel Cave who made a number of very helpful suggestions as to sources and who, as always, has undertaken a thorough review of this work; Derek Butler and other staff of the Commonwealth War Graves Commission at Maidenhead; John Baker of The Map Shop in Upton-upon-Severn who kindly supplied a number of IGN maps; Geoff Thomas has walked many miles of the Somme battlefield in all sorts of weather with me and in his company the sun has always seemed to shine kindly. Major John Rogerson of The Princess of Wales's Royal Regiment and Queen's Regimental Museum. Tony Sprason and the Trustees of the Lancashire Fusiliers Museum. Colonel M.J.Dudding and the Trustees of the 58th Division BEF Memorial Trust Fund. Peter Hart of the IWM has been enormously helpful in allowing me access to his collection of divisional histories and allowing me to stay in London for little more than the price of a couple of pints of beer. Or was it three! The staff at the Public Records Office in Kew have provided me with much help, assistance and considered judgement. Barrie Thorpe, the Western Front Association's memorials officer, has been a particular help to my researches. Many other members of the Western Front Association have also helped in greatly enhancing my knowledge of the Somme battlefield area. To all of these people I should like to extend my sincere thanks whilst making clear that any errors which remain within the text are solely of my own making.

Sensible equipment and advice for visitors

This guide is all about getting outside and walking the battlefields. The walks I have described should never take more than two hours. Nevertheless, to do it you need the right sort of equipment. Sun cream and drinks are absolutely essential, especially in hot weather. Stout shoes or boots in any season are vital. Soon after rain the Somme mud can be glutinous! Always carry appropriate outer clothing. For those of you intent on spending a full day here in the field and who want to record your visit carefully some further items are advisable. Take a sandwich, a camera, a pen and notebook to record where you took your photographs and perhaps to note your visit in the cemetery registers. A pair of binoculars would be helpful, especially in a location such as Maltz Horn Farm where the views are especially extensive. Finally, a decent penknife with a corkscrew, a first aid kit and a small rucksack capable of carrying everything comfortably should complete your requirements. There are many sheltering woodlands across this area, and nearby villages abound where delicious bread, cheeses and a tomato can be found for a perfect lunch. South of Albert on the banks of the Somme at Etinehem, Chipilly or Sailly Laurette there are wonderful places to laze away an afternoon on the south facing slopes above the watercourse.

As I have said in every previous book in this series, here on the Somme a metal detector is, let us be frank, an embarrassment. Many people come here to the fields to sweep for any remnants of clothing, perhaps the occasional Manchester or Liverpool Pals' shoulder title, or whatever. But in my opinion they are better left to rest and await a

Take Care! Even in a new millennium the battlefields of 1918 still give up a steady supply of unstable and potentially deadly munitions.

chance discovery. To be seen digging within sight of what should be places of tranquillity and reflection is almost to desecrate the memory of those whose names are recorded so starkly on those bare white headstones in nearby cemeteries. The spectacle of lone Britons sweeping their electronic plates across empty fields fills me with sadness. This should be a place where a more rewarding and meaningful history reveals itself, without recourse to indignity.

No significant preparation is required to cope with medical requirements. It is sensible to ensure that you carry an E111 form giving reciprocal rights to medical and hospital treatment in France. The necessary documents can be obtained free from any main post office. Ensure that your tetanus vaccination is up to date. Comprehensive personal and vehicle insurance is always advisable abroad.

To help arrange and plan your stay I have identified a list of B&B accommodation and hotels, within easy travelling distances, in Chapter 1 which deals with the designated area today.

How to use this book:

Read it. Go there and walk the area. Take this book, some trench maps and the IGN maps with you. This guide can be used anywhere. However, the area covered is extensive. Within previous guides I have suggested that by far the best way to see the relevant area is on foot or bicycle. In the context of 1918 I have to admit that a car is a bonus. I have suggested some tours in the last chapter, for cars or coaches, as the best way to become familiar with the area's main features. These tours use roads which are easily accessible and will prove quite satisfactory for coaches, involving no dangerous turns through 180°! The tours are strongly recommended to those of you not already conversant with the area. Please note that some of the tracks and smaller roads to be found on the IGN maps of the area are not suitable for coaches. However, none of the tours for cars and coaches I have suggested will take you into such difficulties! When you've done the tours do the walks. Be prepared to leave your car and walk anywhere is the best advice I can give, but take care to lock all valuables, especially cameras and other inviting items, out of sight in the boot of your vehicle if you intend to leave it in an isolated location. However, please do ensure that your car does not block the road or track - these routes can be busy with agricultural traffic, for which, after all, they were built in the first place!

On the subject of Maps.

A compass is an essential companion to any map in the field. I have identified here the maps which appear within this guide. For most navigational and walking purposes these will be more than sufficient for your enjoyment of this area. The area covered by this guide is mapped on no less than seven IGN 1:25000 series sheets. Those maps which cover the 1916 battlefield area are 2408 est, Bray-sur-Somme, 2408 ouest, Albert, 2407 Bapaume est and 2407 Bapaume ouest. To deal with August and early September 1918 you should add 2508 ouest Peronne and 2507 ouest to your collection as well as 2308 est for the Hallue Valley. Taken together these seven maps cover the entirety of the British sector of the 1918 battlefield on the Somme and constitute an indispensable addition to this book in the field. For general access to the area of the Somme sheet 4 in the 1:100,000 IGN green series, Laon and Arras, is very useful. Such maps, and many others covering the entire area of the Western Front, can be obtained by post from The Map Shop in Upton-upon-Severn (01684 593146) or from Waterstones' Booksellers who maintain another excellent specialist map department in Manchester.

However, for a really intimate knowledge of each location the 1:10,000 and 1:5,000 trench maps are indispensable to the serious student or expert. 1;10,000 maps approximate to a scale of six inches to the mile. In order to gain detailed understanding a trench map is therefore indispensable but it is worth noting that the mobile nature of 1918's fighting means that most available maps are 1:20,000 scale.

You should note that the trench maps, which are available from the Imperial War Museum Department of Printed Books (Tel: 0171 416 5348) or the cartographer of the Western Front Association (members only), follow a specific sequence and should be referred to by the numbers usually found in their top right hand corner. Because of the size of the area covered by this guide there are a number of relevant trench maps belonging to the 1:10,000 trench map series. Those are sheet 57cSW3, entitled Longueval, which covers the villages of Longueval and Bazentin-le-Petit, Ginchy, Guillemont and Montauban; and sheet 62cNW1, entitled Maricourt, which covers Maltz Horn Farm, Maricourt, Hardecourt-aux-Bois and the area towards the River Somme. Variously dated versions are available from both sources. In the text I have sometimes referred to locations which are noted on such trench maps, but not on present day maps. In such cases I have where necessary given the relevant trench map reference to help you identify

Trenches and shell-holes in Newfoundland Park.

the exact position. For example, 'Tara Redoubt' on Tara Hill north-east of Albert was located on sheet 57dSE4, at reference W.24.d.5,3.

There are already two museums of note in the vicinity, and an area of preserved battlefield at Newfoundland Park two miles north-west of Thiepval. Some understanding of the ordinary soldiers' lot can be obtained from the Musee des Abris, at Albert below the celebrated Basilica. The second museum, the Historial at Peronne, is well worth travelling to. Take the D938 running south-east from Albert which follows much of the course of the fighting during the August of 1918. Unfortunately the mobile nature of the last 100 day's fighting are not really reflected in the nature of these museums and parks. The new Millennium may well see further developments, which will greatly enhance the experience of visitors, at Thiepval.

One extraordinary fact about the Somme and Ancre battlefield is that after the devastation of the Great War many of the tracks and other features were reconstructed with an uncanny accuracy to their pre-war locations. Most detail shown on trench maps still stand true today. This makes using trench maps in the field easy and pleasurably informative, but we should remember that the Somme is a working community whose roots are based in centuries of toil on the land which is also our place of interest. This is not open access land on the National Trust model. For the sake of good humour and to retain the goodwill which we enjoy be aware of the numerous interests and needs of the farmers and shooting parties, especially in the late summer and autumn months. The farmers will not welcome the sight of your tramping the fields with little regard to germinating seedlings and ripening crops. Please ask before you enter. Please keep to the paths and the edges of each field.

Chapter One

OUR DESIGNATED AREA TODAY

Much of the area described in this guide and known to thousands of British visitors as 'The Somme' is usually associated with the straight road which runs from Albert to Bapaume, the D929, along which it had been planned to execute the 'Big Push' of 1916. However, this book is concerned with the events of late 1918 within which context the River Somme, ten kilometres to the south, is certainly the more influential feature. 1918's events were fought out across great tracts of land, a significant part of which lie west, south and east of the old 1916 battlefield. In those fluid and incredible weeks during August and September of that year the eighteen and nineteen year old soldiers made advances of which their predecessors could only have dreamed. The Official History summarises by saying that:

> 'The progress made by the British Armies, an average of 25 miles on a front of 40 miles, between the 8th August and. the 26th September, fifty days, but mostly in the period 21st August to 18th September, twenty-nine days, had exceeded the expectation and hopes of the troops concerned, accustomed as the older hands were to small gains of ground at great cost. At the Somme the average advance had been only 8 miles on a 12-mile front in 4¹/₂ months. The British casualties in the 1916 battle had been roughly 420,000; in the fighting of 8th August-26th September 1918, about 180,000. The advance had been frontal over country which had been the scene of the Battles of the Somme in 1916, of the German retreat to the Hindenburg Position in 1917, and of the great German offensive of March 1918. The ground, besides being traversed by the south-north course of the Somme and the Canal du Nord, and affording a multitude of small features and localities suitable for concealment of men and guns, was seamed with the trenches and wire of former positions, which furnished a succession of lines admirably suited to an enemy carrying out a series of delaying actions.
>
> Very heavy casualties had been inflicted on the enemy; unlike in all previous offensives, a very large number of prisoners taken, and the enemy had not at his disposal sufficient reinforcements to make the depleted units up to establishment again, nor sufficient reserves to give the tired and fought-out divisions rest, or even sufficient sleep.'[1]

The keys to our understanding of the August 1918 battlefield are the two towns of Amiens and Albert. Albert was familiar to almost every British soldier who had served there during the first Battle of the Somme. By the time that Albert was again fought for, in the autumn of 1918, it was a mere shadow of its former self, a place where the last vestiges of pre-war importance had been reduced to rubble. Today Albert describes itself as being only the '3eme Ville de la Somme', but quite properly 'la Cite d'Ancre'. The Town Hall square in Albert often hosts a market and there are three small supermarkets nearby which can provide an array of food and refreshments. The area due east of Albert is familiar to all who have studied and walked the 1916 battlefields. But the fine history of Morlancourt ridge, south of Albert, is often overlooked by people intent only upon 1916. South of Fricourt, towards Bray-sur-Somme, is a vast open area of downland which was the scene of much severe fighting during the Battle of Albert in the autumn of 1918[2]. East of the 1916 area the numerous villages see fewer visitors than do well known locations such as Mansel Copse at Mametz or Lochnagar crater at La Boisselle, yet the story of the crossing of the Canal du Nord is one which should inspire anyone interested in the history of the Great War.

To the west of Albert is a wonderful and relatively unvisited area, full of interest and set in some of the most picturesque scenery. The countryside is scattered with numerous British cemeteries many of which have a strong link with 1918. The land runs back across uplands before falling away into the lovely valley of the River Hallue where Rawlinson's headquarters was located within Querrieu chateau. Much of this area is well behind the British lines, even after the German advances in the spring of 1918. Here many graves mark lives cut short just weeks before the end of the war.

There are relatively few hotels within this area and the first thing you might need to arrange is accommodation and tomorrow morning's

Albert in the late summer of 1918, 'a mere shadow of its former self'.

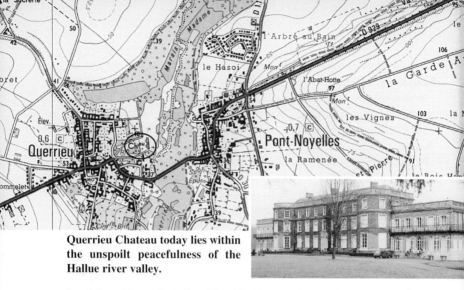

Querrieu Chateau today lies within the unspoilt peacefulness of the Hallue river valley.

breakfast. I have therefore identified below some of the nearby hotels and a number of B&B houses where you can base yourself during a visit.

B&B style accommodation

Auchonvillers – Beaumont Hamel. Comfortable and well appointed accommodation for up to eight people. Attractive grounds and interesting walks nearby. Evening meals and continental breakfast. Towards the northern end of the area covered by this guide. Mike and Julie Renshaw. Les Galets. Route de Beaumont, Auchonvillers. Tel: 03.22.76.28.79.

Auchonvillers. Five good rooms with en suite facilities and an interesting history, the centrepiece of which is the cellar still carved with the names of many soldiers who passed through in 1916. Bed, breakfast and evening meals by arrangement as well as a room for non residents. Again, towards the northern end of the area covered by this guide. Avril Williams. 10 Rue Delattre, 80560 Auchonvillers. Tel: 03.22.76.23.66.

Hardecourt-aux-Bois. Newly renovated and well appointed accommodation. This is a fine location and a comfortable house, with three en-suite bedrooms, situated in a tranquil Somme village just to the south of the British 1916 sector. Perfectly situated for a 1918 tour. Evening meals by request. A three bedroom chalet, which sleeps up to eight people is available for those of you wishing to self-cater. Vic and Dianne Piuk. Les Allouettes, 10 Rue du Mantier, 80360, Hardecourt-aux-Bois. Tel: 03.22.85.14.56.

Martinpuich. A welcoming and comfortable house which can cater for up to eight people. This newly renovated house is situated at the heart of the Somme battlefields providing excellent and speedy access to most areas dealt with in this guide. Evening meals by request and continental breakfast. Colin and Lisa Gillard. 54 Grand Rue, Martinpuich, 62450 Bapaume. Tel: 03.21.50.18.87.

Camping:

The Bellevue campsite in Authuille is a fine and central point on the Somme battlefield. The site is quiet and often frequented by people who share an interest in the Great War. The owner, Monsieur Desailly, and his family are always welcoming. During 1998 Monsieur Desailly also opened an excellent self catering facility on site in a well appointed cottage style flat which is fully equipped to cater for a number of people in comfort. Here you are within two minute's walk of the Authuille Military Cemetery and not far from the Auberge de la Vallee d'Ancre on the banks of the River Ancre. For many years this bar and restaurant has served decent food and drinks for as long as you cared to stay! The Auberge is owned by Denis Bourgoyne who has already established a fine reputation for the quality of his food amongst the local community.

There are numerous campsites in the valley of the river Somme south of the Morlancourt ridge and in the Ancre valley south-west of Albert. However, it can be bitterly cold camping in February! Therefore, for those of you who are travelling in style or during these colder and wetter months of the year, a roof over your heads may be welcome. The list identified below may be of some help, but it should not be inferred that the order is one of descending merit! To call for reservations from the UK dial 00 33, followed by the 9 digit number. In all these hotels, with one exception in Picquigny, you will find at least one person on the hotel's staff who can speak English.

Hotels:

The Grande Hotel de la Paix *, 43 Rue Victor Hugo, 80300 Albert. Tel (0033) 03.22.75.01.64.

The Hotel de la Basilique **, 3 - 5 Rue Gambetta, 80300 Albert. Tel (0033)03.22.75.04.71.

The Relais Fleuri **, 56 Avenue Faidherbe, 80300 Albert. Tel (0033)03.22.75.08.11.

Les Etangs du Levant *, Rue du 1er Septembre, 80340 Bray sur Somme. Tel (0033)03.22.76.70.00.

Auberge de Picquigny **, 112 Rue du 60 R.I., 80310 Picquigny. Tel (0033)03.22.51.20.53.

Hotel Le Prieure. 17 Route National, 80860 Rancourt. Tel (0033)03.22.85.04.43.

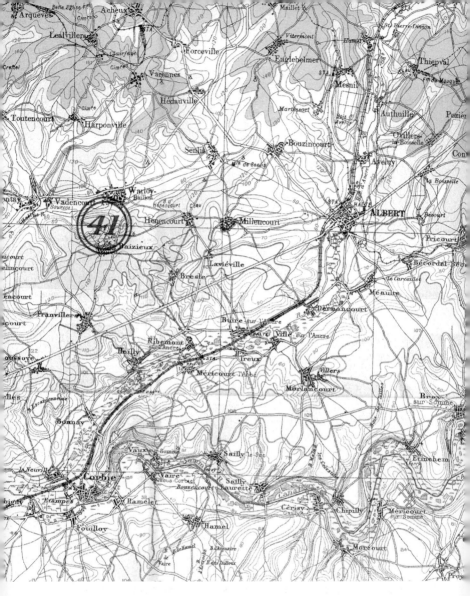

The Area covered by this guide.

Once you are established it is time to see the surrounding locality and I suggest that, soon after you arrive, you would enjoy following the general tour explained in Chapter 6. However, in this first chapter I have attempted to give some definition to the boundaries of this guidebook and give a brief commentary to illustrate the importance of the area's history.

The places within this guide which form a starting point to

18

Map. Detail from the 1:100,000 sheet within the Official History (France & Belgium 1918, Vol 1. Sheet 1) showing the area covered by this guide. Although drawn in 1932, by the Ordnance Survey's Historical Section, almost all of the roads shown here still hold good today.

understanding the area would be the front lines in the vicinities of the Sailly villages on the north bank of the Somme and thence across the ridge towards Ville-sur-Ancre. West of Albert towards the picturesque valley of the River Hallue the villages of Franvillers, Lavieville, Henencourt, Millencourt and Bouzincourt are filled with interest and history from the period prior to the events of August 1918. These positions had been defined by the limit of the German spring offensive which had been halted in this area on the west of Albert by the 35th (Bantam)[3] Division as well as the 3rd and 4th Australian Divisions. Here were trenches named by and after the many Australians who served in this vicinity before August 1918, Melbourne Trench, Dinkum Avenue and Canberra Trench. Many Australian gunners who died during this period are buried within Frechencourt Communal Cemetery in the beautiful Hallue valley to the west. This whole area is the site of a number of military cemeteries and small communal cemetery extensions which are only infrequently visited. Typically, on the upland plateau west of Albert, is Lavieville[4] whose communal cemetery contains six Australians killed during April 1918 as well as the graves of an artilleryman from the 1917 fighting and a soldier killed during the Second World War, in 1944. Another and more sizeable cemetery is the Millencourt communal cemetery extension. This contains many graves from the spring fighting in 1918. Not far away is the interesting village of Henencourt which was an important billet in the period prior to 1916's fighting. Amongst many other units, the Salford Pals were here. It has an imposing chateau, part of which has been destroyed by shellfire, and it is still the site of four substantial pillboxes which were built by British engineers belonging to the 47th

Franvillers Communal Cemetery Extension. Here are many Australian servicemen's graves from the summer of 1918. One grave which caught my eye was that of Private Thomas Harrison, 28th Bn. Australian Infantry. Although serving with Australian forces he was the son of Leon and Elizabeth Harrison who came from the picturesque village of Tideswell, near Buxton in Derbyshire, England. A search of the CWGC web site therefore fails to bring up his records under 'Nationality: UK and Former Colonies'!

(London) Division in the summer of 1918. Half a mile west of the village there was a sizeable military cemetery, Henencourt Wood, the graves within which were removed to Ribemont, in the Ancre valley, after the war. In addition Henencourt's communal cemetery originally contained 35 graves from the 1918 period which were also later removed to Ribemont.

By the summer of 1918 the British had concentrated huge amounts of artillery across this plateau of elevated ground west of Albert. Large siege batteries were surrounded by 4.5' and 18 pounder units. During July and early August most of the siege units based here had targets on the Morlancourt Ridge, south of the River Ancre. One team of gunners with 309 Siege Battery, attached to the 25th and 12th Divisions at various times that year, were here in the early summer of 19185. Their position was 100 yards south of Lavieville, close to the main Albert to Amiens road. Writing in 1919 one of their number recounted how a number of the older inhabitants of the village were reluctant to leave, even in the face of appalling danger.

'Battered and broken, indeed, it appeared as one went to seek wood or straw in it - bricks lying along its quiet little streets, thin fingers of lath and rafter sticking forth from the side of some ruined house. And through those terrible times three aged people refused to leave their homes. Jumbo Symes one day was wandering about the village, and called to me, cautiously approaching the place, to talk to an old lady whom he had just seen in the garden. She invited us inside her house. The glass of the windows had already been shattered, and the loose tiles shaken off the roof. By the stove sat her husband, a weak old man, whom the ever-threatening danger seemed to have practically paralysed, for he sat quite speech\-less. He was a tailor, and on a counter lay his cloth and scissors; the room was well kept, and Madame was tidying it up while we were there. These little articles of peaceful life, this feminine clinging to the care and orderliness of the home, how infinitely pathetic they seemed in their futility now, when a shell might at any moment sweep all to oblivion! We asked Madame why they would not flee. "Non, non, m'sieu', nous sommes trop vieux pour partir: il nous faut rester ici." Even while we were drinking coffee with them there came that terrible roar through the air, that earth-shaking explosion. The poor little lady clutched convulsively at us. The window-shutters, which had been fastened up, were thrown open by the burst. Yet before the debris had well finished falling on the

house, Madame was outside, fixing up the shutters again. We looked at the great eight-inch shell-hole less than thirty yards away, and left the tragic old couple, sadly wondering whether Providence would so marvellously preserve them through following days. They were eventually evacu\-ated, so we heard, but the third old person was found dead in a cellar.'[6]

Walking into Lavieville today from the direction of the Amiens road it is easy to visualise the scene. In summer the coolness of the plateau make it a refreshing respite from the heat of the valleys. In winter it is an exposed and bleak place.

The exposed plateau west of Albert is home to a number of interesting and intimate cemeteries. This is Lavieville communal cemetery from which there are extensive views across Albert and the British positions held in the summer of 1918.

It was from this area, before the Battle of Amiens began on 8 August, that the Australian Corps were moved to new positions south of the River Somme and British divisions came to be concentrated north of the river on the left flank of the Amiens battlefront. To help identify these positions and to orientate yourself here just west of Albert, on the D929 Amiens road, there is a Demarcation Stone purporting to mark the limits of the German's spring advance. The stone lies about 1 kilometre from the town centre at a railway bridge which spans a deep cutting. Beneath the bridge there was a series of deep German dugouts forming shelters for their soldiers in support of front line units. However, a more appropriate position for the stone would be the westernmost positions reached by the Germans, 500 metres to the west in the direction of Amiens, by the woods on the left of the road.

Within this book I have included the sphere of operations undertaken by both V Corps of the Third Army and the Fourth Army north of the Somme during the August of 1918, up to early September that year by when the fighting had moved further east, away from the Somme battlefield. The southern boundary of this guide is formed by

22

The Demarcation Stone south-west of Albert on the D929 where the road crosses the railway. The larger photograph shows the view eastwards from the railway bridge towards the town centre. There is another well preserved Demarcation Stone in the area of Ville sur Ancre.

the presence of Australian units and/or the River Somme at the Battle of Amiens. That battle was a joint initiative undertaken by the French First Army and the British Fourth Army. The French advance is often referred to as the Battle of Montdidier, 1918. On the far right of the British Fourth Army were the 3rd and 1st Canadian divisions and then to their left the 2nd and 3rd Australian divisions. The operations of that

Map: An original trench map showing the exact location of the German and British positions west of Albert astride the Amiens road. The map, although rather faded, is clearly corrected to 23/6/1918.

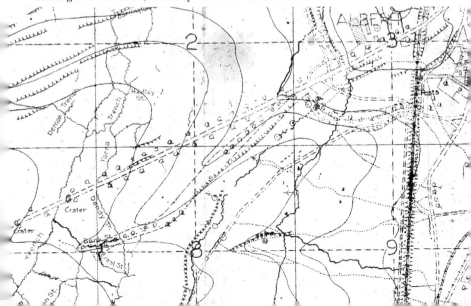

The date is 8 August, 1918, the first day of the Battle of Amiens. The location is Sailly-le-Sec in the Somme Valley, just behind the initial British front lines facing towards Sailly-Laurette where the German front lines had just been breached. Already there are many wounded and German prisoners collecting at this Aid Post.

3rd Australian division therefore form the southern limit of this guide since the division's left flank lay on the River Somme. As the Battle of Amiens was developed in the first few hours after zero, 4.20 am on 8th August, the villages of Sailly Laurette[7], Cerisy, Chipilly and Morlancourt came to figure in the fighting at the north of Fourth Army's operations. That northern sector of Fourth Army was III Corps' sphere of operations, within which the 58th, 18th and 12th Divisions

The eastern boundary of the guide – the Canal du Nord between the villages of Moislains and Ytres.

were engaged. During the next 48 hours the villages of Dernancourt and Morlancourt, south-west of Albert, also fell.

The northern boundary of this guide will be a line running roughly west-east from Beaumont Hamel to Warlencourt, that is to include V Corps' area of operations during the Battle of Albert to the north of Fourth Army. The Battle of Albert was engaged on 21st August. V Corps' troops in that battle were part of Third Army. The eastern limit of this guide is found at the banks of the Canal du Nord between the villages of Moislains and Ytres. Before the advances made by the German Army during the spring of 1918 the British battle positions had lain just a few miles east of this canal. In essence then this book covers the Battle of Amiens, in so far as the British Army were involved, the recapture of Albert and then deals with the final ejection of the German army from the bulk of the 1916 Somme battlefield during late August 1918. By 29th August the advance undertaken by the British had taken them to Bapaume. One week's fighting in 1918 had crossed a battlefield which, in the summer of 1916, had provided stalemate for four and a half months of intense conflict.

In order to help visualise the topography of these events any guide would be well advised to take his or her students to a number of fine vantage points from which a great deal of the 1918 battlefield can be seen. I have listed below a small number of favourites viewpoints.

Viewpoints:

• Bonte Redoubt. This location, in the spring of 1916, was the most important of the British artillery observation posts on the southern arm of their frontage. Bonte Redoubt was located south of the Albert - Peronne road, half way between Becordel-Becourt and Fricourt. It gives a very fine view northwards across the village of Becourt towards La Boisselle, and eastwards across Fricourt, Mametz and onwards towards Maricourt, Montauban and Trones Wood. This view covers the advance of the 18th Division following the Battle of Albert.

• The Grandstand. This was the scene of a visit by General Rawlinson on the morning of 1 July 1916. Rawlinson came to witness the opening shots of the Battle of the Somme that terrible day. The location however provides a fine panorama of much of the 1918 battlefield. It can be reached from Dernancourt by following the D52 in the direction of Buire sur l'Ancre. Turn right under the railway bridge in the direction of Millencourt and pass the British military cemetery on your left, proceeding uphill for one kilometre, ignoring the first track on your right, past a small copse on your right. Take the farm track on the right about 150 metres past the copse and follow the track until the view becomes extensive at the point where the track turns sharply to the right. This is the Grandstand.

• Bouzincourt Ridge Cemetery. This is a superior vantage point from which to view the 1918 fighting in the Ancre Valley north of Albert towards Thiepval. In my opinion this is the best of the view points described within this guide. The cemetery can be reached from the D20 road between Bouzincourt and Aveluy although the track to the cemetery is very rough and generally impassable in winter and wet weather. A better approach is from the Albert to Aveluy road where that road crosses the main railway line outside Albert. Travelling from Albert cross the bridge and turn immediately left. After two hundred

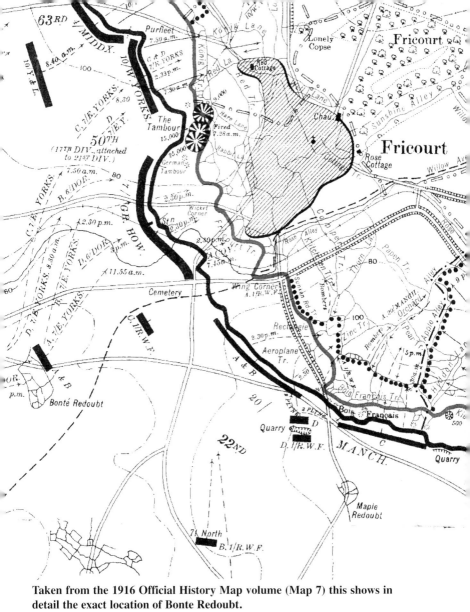

Taken from the 1916 Official History Map volume (Map 7) this shows in
detail the exact location of Bonte Redoubt.
Part of the view across Fricourt from the area close to Bonte Redoubt.

The view towards Thiepval Ridge from Bouzincourt Ridge Cemetery.

metres turn right and begin to rise up the lower slopes of the Bouzincourt ridge. After 1 kilometre take the left fork and the cemetery is a further 500 metres on your left.

• Dantzig Alley Cemetery. This is also a fine location from which to visualise events relating to August 1918 and especially the parts played by the 18th Division Dantzig Alley cemetery is to be found just to the east of the village of Mametz in the direction of Montauban on the D64 road. The cemetery receives relatively few visitors considering its size, importance and location but you will find that the panoramic views available here are well worth a detour. Those views are interesting in that the 18th Division passed this way twice - once in 1916 a little to the east during their attacks on 1st July across Pommiers Redoubt, and once in 1918 but this time in an easterly direction. The rear of the cemetery also looks out over terrain familiar to the 38th Division's men - that of 1916 during their terrible baptism of fire at Mametz Wood and

The crucifix at Maltz Horn farm with Trones Wood to the north.

also in 1918 as they crossed the north of that wood heading east on the northern flank of the 18th Division. There are a small number of graves from the autumn of 1918, but the vast majority of the 2,500 graves date from 1916.

• Maltz Horn Farm. Maltz Horn farm, once the home of Maltzkorn Duclerq, was utterly destroyed during the 1916 fighting south of Trones Wood. Today its location is defined by a prominent crucifix. The site possesses one of the finest all-round panoramic vistas anywhere on the Somme battlefield, southwards across Hardecourt-aux-Bois towards the Somme, northwards past Trones Wood towards Longueval and Delville Wood and eastwards across Guillemont towards Leuze Wood. The location is to the south of Trones Wood on the road running towards Hardecourt.

• Pozieres and the Windmill. This is the highest point on the 1916 battlefield and is located just east of Pozieres on the Albert - Bapaume road. From here you can see across Pozieres towards Albert in the west as well as north-westwards across the Thiepval - Pozieres ridge. To the north-east lie Courcelette, Le Sars and Bapaume whilst to the south and south-east is much of the upland and the great horseshoe of woods associated with the events of early autumn 1916. During 1999 an elevated viewing platform was erected at the site of the Gibraltar observation post, west of Pozieres, from which uninterrupted views can be obtained across Albert and beyond Thiepval.

The view across the site of the Windmill, above Pozieres, towards Thiepval. An alternative location to view can be found at the elevated platform at the Gibraltar position west of Pozieres.

The view across the Ancre valley towards Hamel and Newfoundland Park from the site of the Ulster Tower. In the foreground is the Orange Order memorial which was removed during 1999.

• The village of Thiepval. The Memorial to the Missing is not a good vantage point because of the proximity of too many trees. However, within half a mile there are numerous places from which extensive views can be had. That from the nearby Ulster Tower northwards across the Ancre valley towards Beaumont Hamel and north eastwards towards Hamel is especially worthwhile if you are considering the role of V Corps during the early days of the Battle of Albert around the northern limits of this guide.

• The banks of the River Somme in this area include two outstanding viewpoints. The first is the Chipilly ridge. This is a beautiful area with magnificent views. The ridge was attacked by the 58th Division on 9 August. Beneath the ridge within the picturesque village is the memorial to the 58th Division's men. Further upstream lies the hamlet of Vaux on the banks of the Somme east of Suzanne. The area east of Bray-sur-Somme around the villages of Suzanne, Vaux and Curlu on the banks of the Somme's meandering and leisurely progress is also both picturesque and historically interesting. Suzanne has a fascinating chateau and the walk from there to Vaux is full of interest for the visitor interested in both 1916 and 1918's events. Above Vaux there is a fine vantage point overlooking the river. The 3rd Australian division were here on 27th August 1918 before their advance continued past Curlu towards Clery-sur-Somme.

• The Australian memorial at Villers Bretonneux. Although this lies to the immediate south of the town of Corbie, above the southern banks of the River Somme, the remarkable memorial allows some of the best views along the river and across the Morlancourt Ridge to the north. Although this is slightly outside the scope of this guide I do strongly recommend that you visit this place. It is especially perfect at evening when the low sun is to the west, revealing the folds and slopes of the area's topography beautifully. The elevated central tower can be ascended by a series of internal steps which eventually culminate in an enclosed viewing platform with directional arrows towards significant landmarks. To access this site from the area of

The viewing platform and orientation table within the tower at the Australian memorial at Villers Bretonneux.

Villers Bretonneux memorial seen from Corbie Communal Cemetery extension.

this guide head south, across the River Somme on the D23 towards Villers Bretonneux, from Corbie. The memorial is on your left as you approach the high ground astride the ridge. It is one location where a pair of binoculars are indispensable.

Which cemeteries and memorials?

Within this area are untold numbers of cemeteries and memorials. It is unnecessary to include those which are specific to the fighting which took place in earlier years and before the summer of 1918. The best known of these is the Thiepval Memorial to the Missing. A fine example of a 1915-16 battlefield cemeteries would be that at Authuille. However, this area does include a number of cemeteries and memorials which are specific to the August - September 1918 period and a further group which include reference to men and events from other periods as well as August - September 1918. Perhaps the most problematic are those cemeteries which are the result, in great part, of the concentration of graves and bodies which were discovered during the post war years. As a rule I have included those cemeteries where the fighting which occurred during August - September 1918 has given rise to a significant proportion of a cemetery's graves.

1. Official History. Military Operations. France and Belgium. 1918. Vol IV.

2. A footnote in the Official History tries to make clear the way in which these events have been named. 'The official Battle Nomenclature gives: 'The Second Battles of the ' 'Somme 1918' 21st August-3rd September, with the subheadings 'Battle of Albert 1918' 21st-23rd August, with the tactical incident of the capture of Chuignes 23rd August; and 'The Second Battle of Bapaume' 31st August-3rd September, with the tactical incident of the capture of Mont St. Quentin, and the occupation of Peronne but the Somme title for 1918 has never come into use, being reserved for 1916, and the Battle of Albert did not end until the 29th August.'

3. Established in 1915 as a unit for men of small stature, but now, by 1918, accommodating soldiers of all heights and sizes.

4. Spelt as 'La Vieville' in the CWGC registers and information. Cemetery index number Fr.199.

5. Battery were equipped with 6' guns.

6. *London Gunners. The Story of the HAC Siege Battery in Action* . Kingham. Methuen & Co. 1919.

7. Sailly Laurette is sometimes spelt as Sailly Lorette on British Official History Maps.

8. These are covered in great detail within the pages of other guides in this series.

Chapter Two

THE SITUATION UP TO EARLY AUGUST 1918

On 21 March of 1918 the German army launched its spring offensive between the Sensee and Oise rivers. The impact of that offensive, born from the collapse of Russian participation in the war, had been dramatic[1]. The British Army had been pushed back across the old 1916 Somme battlefield from their positions facing St.Quentin. As the end of March approached the British had lost control of Albert and were clinging to positions south and west of the town. The 38th Welsh Division were brought south from Armentieres on 2nd April to support the exhausted 2nd and 47th Divisions which were holding the lines between Albert and Hamel. Thus began an association with the Somme battlefield which was to last until September and would later see the 38th Division re-cross almost the entirety of the 1916 battlefields. Of those two exhausted divisions the 2nd left but the 47th stayed and also forged an important link with the history of the advance to victory during August and early September here on the Somme.

The German spring offensive was a catalyst; the moment when potentially disastrous circumstances ensured that the Franco-British conference at Doullens would have to face up to the situation's

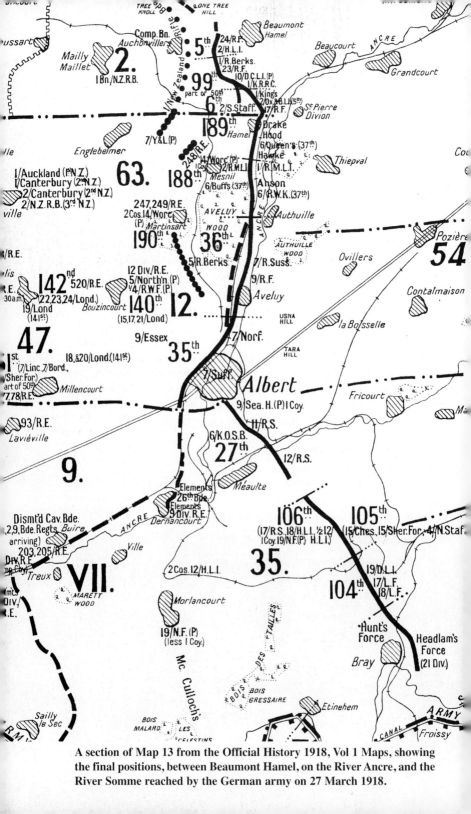

A section of Map 13 from the Official History 1918, Vol 1 Maps, showing the final positions, between Beaumont Hamel, on the River Ancre, and the River Somme reached by the German army on 27 March 1918.

seriousness and agree the terms of a greater unity of command[2]. By the time that the fighting in the vicinity of Albert died away, at the end of the first week in April, the expenditure of men, munitions and materials by the German armed forces during this period had been enormous. Later, on 9 April, the German Army would launch another offensive in the area of the River Lys around La Bassee and Armentieres. This fighting would last until 29 April. A further German offensive was later developed on the River Aisne between Soissons and Reims, beginning on 27 May and lasting until 2 June. On 9 June another significant German effort was launched between Noyon and Montdidier south of the Somme. However, the last and potentially most telling German offensive was launched on 15 July when the Second Battle of the Marne began. Three days later an enormous allied counter attack by both French and American troops succeeded in reversing German advances and regaining vast tracts of territory in the Champagne region. This exhausting battle was effectively over by 4 August.

The Demarcation Stone just outside the village of Ville-sur-Ancre on the D120 road towards Meaulte. British troops of the 35th (Bantam) Division were involved in halting the German advance in this area although the stone's location is somewhat deceptive since the initial German front lines were a little west of this junction. *(Map - Tour 2a)*

Here lay the roots of Germany's final defeat. In these last desperate throws of the dice in the hope of defeating the allies before the impact of American troops came to overwhelm the German army, Ludendorff

US artillerymen fire on German positions using a French 75mm field gun

had come to overstretch his available resources. By 14 April, following the Doullens conference, Foch was appointed Commander in Chief of the allied armies in France giving a degree of unity and purpose to overall strategy on the Western Front. The results of this change could not be immediate. Nevertheless, in the forthcoming four months a series of disparate actions, some defensive and some localised attacks, undertaken by both the French and British would further undermine German strength. One typical small action within the area of this guide was at Ville-sur-Ancre where the Australians recaptured the village south-west of Albert on 18 May.

Foch, Commander in Chief of the allied armies.

Part of the problem facing the British and French allies was the disruption to their transport infrastructure caused by the German's advance. The maximum penetration which the German army achieved was between St.Quentin and Villers Bretonneux. A significant consequence of that German advance was that the three main railway lines emanating from the east of Amiens

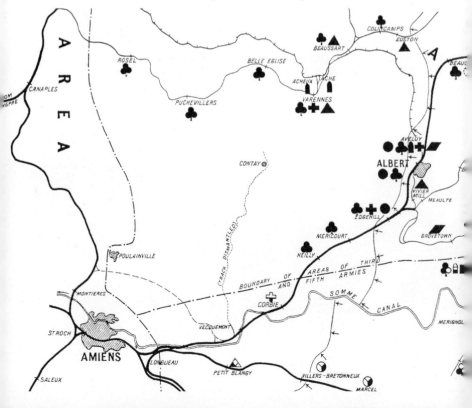

were either captured in their entirety or cut. The loss of a section of the Amiens - Arras line to the north of Albert meant that during the late spring and throughout the summer of 1918 British troop movements between Arras and the Albert area had to be undertaken via circuitous routes through St.Pol and Doullens.

By late July the French and American successes at the Second Battle of the Marne had drawn many German reserves away from the British frontage. At the end of that month British intelligence reported that of the 201 remaining German divisions 106 were classed as temporarily unfit, because of the impact of recent fighting. Further, the quality of German troops was being undermined by outbreaks of disease, especially chest infections. British troops reported that some of their German opponents were reluctant to engage in localised combat, patrols or any form of offensive actions. As if to confirm their shrinking resources the establishment of every German battalion was reduced in strength from 980 to 800 all ranks by 1 July 1918. Fifty four per cent of the recent reinforcements arriving at German front line infantry units had been returned to those units still wounded and 32 per cent were very young soldiers of the 1919 class.

The situation was revealed perfectly in our area when a raid, undertaken by soldiers of the 22nd Londons, 47th Division, on the 24th

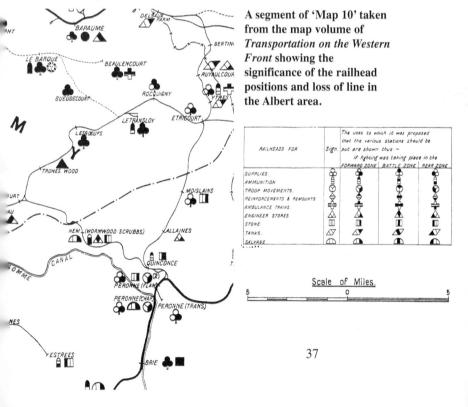

A segment of 'Map 10' taken from the map volume of *Transportation on the Western Front* showing the significance of the railhead positions and loss of line in the Albert area.

37

July entered the German trenches north west of Albert's railway sidings between W.21.d.1.1 and W.21.d.4.5. *(Map - Tour 1a)*. The Germans fled in terror and many German soldiers of 450 I.R. (233rd Division) were killed by Lewis gun fire. Two were taken prisoner for interrogation. The subsequent Intelligence Summary is revealing:

The third battalion [of 450 I.R] *(in reserve in railway cutting) is unable to hold the line owing to 'Flanders Grippe' (Influenza)...Enemy wire is very poor, and forms no obstacle of consequence. Patrolling is rarely done by the enemy, and the men appear quite ignorant of the position of our front line and the condition of No Man's Land. No attack by the enemy appears to*

The remains of the railway station at Albert during the 1918 fighting.

be contemplated on this front at present. On the contrary, the men [taken prisoner] *have been told the British are concentrating for an attack on the Albert Front.'* [3]

The condition of the German armies west of Albert and elsewhere in the Somme area was known. They were revealed as exhausted and battle weary. For some time the material flows of war had begun to ebb in the allies favour. Now the less tangible but vital human qualities of British morale and the waning resolve of Germany's armed forces were beginning to reveal themselves. Within those German battalions the proportion of ill prepared and unsuitable soldiers grew inexorably within each unit.

That lack of morale was revealed in one decision, announced in early August, whereby German troops to the west of the River Ancre between Dernancourt and Aveluy Wood, as well as further south to the west of the River Avre and Riviere des Doms between Montdidier and Moreuil, were withdrawn on 3 August. Feeling in the German command structure was that it was undesirable to allow the forward troops to fight with a river close behind them. The following day the German Chief of General Staff, uneasy about this atmosphere of defeatism and lethargy, issued a famous Order of the Day.

'*G.H.Q., 4-8-18*

I am under the impression that, in many quarters, the possibility of an enemy offensive is viewed with a certain degree of apprehension. There is nothing to justify this apprehension, provided our troops are vigilant and do their duty.

In all the open warfare operations in the course of their great offensive battle between the Marne and the Vesle, the French were only able to obtain one initial tactical success due to surprise, namely that of July 18th, and this success ought to have been denied them. In the fighting which followed, the enemy in spite of his mass of artillery, was unable to obtain the slightest tactical advantage; and yet, far from occupying prepared positions, our troops were fighting in open country and were merely holding the positions which they had chanced upon at the end of a day's battle. All the enemy's attacks broke down with sanguinary losses. It was not the enemy's tactical successes which caused our withdrawal, but the precarious state of our rearward communications.

The French and British infantry generally fought with caution; the Americans attacked more boldly but with less skill. It is to the tanks that the enemy owes his success of the first day. These, however, would not have been formidable if the infantry had not allowed itself to be surprised, and if the artillery had been sufficiently distributed in depth. At the present moment, we occupy everywhere positions which have been very strongly fortified, and we have, I am convinced, effected a judicious organisation in depth of the infantry and artillery.

Henceforward, we can await every hostile attack with the greater confidence. As I have already explained, we should wish for nothing better than to see the enemy launch an offensive, which can but hasten the disintegration of his forces.

Commanders and men must be imbued with a bitter determination to conquer, both in the defensive as well as in the offensive. This is a consideration which must not be lost sight of during training. Hence, we must not, in the present circumstances, neglect the organised defensive by devoting ourselves too exclusively to offensive tactics; generally speaking, the organised defensive is the more difficult. It is the latter, in fact, which imposes the greatest test upon the spirit of the troops.
LUDENDORFF'[4]

In this respect circumstances were clearly propitious for an allied attack in the Amiens - Somme area. The scene was set for the Battle of Amiens, beginning on 8th August, the German Army's 'Black Day'.

Part 2: The situation of the British and Allied armies.

Although the British forces in the area west of Albert had taken a tremendous blow during late March, their resolve was demonstrably not broken. Within days of the German advance establishing itself across the Bouzincourt ridge area the British proved determined to contest the position and re-install themselves in places of local tactical advantage where possible. This was not a period of static inactivity. For example, on 12th April the 38th (Welsh) Division was brought into the lines opposite Albert. This unique division had been established as a consequence of Lloyd George's initiative in seeking the establishment of a Welsh Army. During the summer of 1916 the division had experienced a terrible baptism of fire in the Mametz Wood area. Now back on the Somme their experience in April and May was typical of the aggressive stance adopted even though local conditions were far from ideal.

The men found the trenches they took over were hastily made and only partially finished. Sometimes crumbling old trenches dating back to 1914 had been pressed into use. Where the lines ran between Bouzincourt and Aveluy the Germans held the high ground, denying observation into the Ancre Valley. It was decided the 38th should capture this ground while the 35th Division on their left improved the position in Aveluy Wood and the Australians, on the right, lent the assistance of their artillery. The attack took place at 7.30 pm on 22nd April and was undertaken by the 113th Brigade and 2nd Royal Welsh

Fusiliers. Although, because of the strength of the German's position and numerous machine guns and artillery support, the attack did not succeed in driving the enemy completely off the plateau, it did succeed in advancing the 38th's lines a distance of 250 metres on a frontage of 1000 metres and denied the Germans observation of the British lines, a situation which he had previously enjoyed. This localised attack gained a position from where the Ancre Valley could be seen. Two officers and eighty-three other ranks were taken prisoners and six machine guns were captured. Whilst the 38th's divisional history describes these events as 'a decided success' it was a costly operation and some of the attacking companies were reduced to a strength of thirty men. The 13th Royal Welsh Fusiliers, who were on the right, were the most successful in making forward progress but also sustained the greatest number of casualties, eight officers and 263 other ranks. *(Map - Tour 1a)*

It was D Company, under Capt. C.B.Williams, M.C., who reached and held on to their final objective giving observation into the Ancre Valley; this company were heavily counter-attacked the next morning, 23 April, at 4.40 a.m. and again at 7.30 p.m. but held their ground. During the night of the 22/23rd the Field Ambulances evacuated 400 wounded between 7.30 p.m. and 7 a.m. The regimental stretcher bearers were assisted by the Divisional Pioneers after the latter had completed their work of consolidation and Private G.Stewkesbury of that Battalion was awarded the D.C.M. for his gallantry in connection with this. Though wounded in the right eye and nearly blind he continued stretcher bearing until he fainted after being wounded a second time. The Brigade remained on the position that it had won until the night of the 25th when it was relieved by the 115th Brigade and withdrew into reserve close at hand.

Subsequently, on 9th May, the enemy made a determined attack in force against this high ground which he always disputed strongly and which was evidently considered important; at the same time he attacked the Australians on the 38th Division's right, both attacks being preceded by an exceptionally heavy bombardment. The Germans succeeded in driving the Australians back from their front line but the right of the 115th Brigade held by C and D Companies, 17th Royal Welsh Fusiliers, held on all day with their flank exposed until a counter-attack by the Australians restored the situation the next night.

On the 20th May the 38th Division came out of the line for a fortnight's rest after a successful raid had been carried out by the 14th and 16th Royal Welsh Fusiliers on the 18th. On relief that day the

Major-General Blackader meets the monarch during his tour of the Somme area in the August of 1916.

Divisional commander, Major-General Blackader, was hospitalised to the Pasteur Institute in Paris. Three days later, on 23rd May, Major-General T.A.Cubitt, C.M.G. D.S.O., arrived to take command of the Division.

One small insight, most probably apocryphal, was given within the pages of the 18th Division's history. Talking fondly of the 38th (Welsh) division, with which the 18th were to be closely associated throughout the autumn of 1918, the text introduced the new commander. Cubitt's manner was abrupt, direct and much to the liking of the 18th Division's staff, many of his peers and the men under his command. It was said of him when he took command of his new Division that,

> *'it was sorely tried and in need of men* [and] *General Cubitt wrote to Mr Lloyd George for more Welshmen. A strong draft turned up - whether the result of the letter or not General Cubitt does not know. His own description of the success of the appeal - and, as usual, most of his words were unfit for print - was, "The little beggar hadn't the decency to answer my letter; but he sent me the men."* [5]

These men were of course the early waves which later became a flood of eighteen and nineteen year olds in the summer of 1918. During the German spring and early summer offensives the British army had been

(Below) '...a flood of eighteen and nineteen year olds in the summer of 1918.' These men, serving with the Lancashire Fusiliers, were typical of the youth which characterised many men within the British Army during the last few months fighting of 1918.

(Above) Whilst the young men are often remembered as characterising the British Army of 1918 the 40 year old drafts have often been overlooked. In the harsh conditions of mobile warfare such men often suffered terribly. This photograph shows Private Herbert Jones, 2nd Royal Welsh Fusiliers, who died aged 41 on 1 September 1918, near to Morval whilst serving with the 38th Welsh Division. He is buried at Sailly-Saillisel British cemetery.

forced to endure battle conditions of testing severity. But it was also clear, by the time those attacks had lost their impetus, that ultimately the German effort had been exhausted. Now the British could prosper on the back of the old sweat's indomitable spirit, the resilient powers of recovery which the youngsters brought and from the arrival of American assistance. It was also clear that the early 1918 reorganisation of British infantry, into brigades formed of three battalions rather than four, had served to make the Army's command and control structure simpler and more effective. However, numerous

British infantry units were woefully beneath strength, many going into action during August of 1918 with less than 400 of all ranks, but those men's morale had been elevated by the utter failure of the German spring and summer offensives to inflict defeat.

The massive assault on the German positions astride the River Somme, undertaken on 8th August, would be made by the British Fourth Army[6], commanded by Rawlinson, with the French First Army on its right flank, south of the Amiens - Roye road. To clear the way the remaining French inhabitants of the city of Amiens were evacuated by March, since which time the area behind the forthcoming assault was placed under the strictest military control in order to ensure the secrecy of forthcoming British operations. The necessary preparations included a massive build up of supplies which only served to deepen the contrast with German units which were, by measurable material and clear psychological criteria, ill prepared and lacking in resolve to cope with the forthcoming assaults upon their positions.

Behind the British positions, in preparation for the forthcoming battle,

> 'two casualty clearing stations (reinforced by extra surgical teams and nursing sisters) were allotted to each corps for the sick and wounded, together with motor ambulance convoys, advanced depots of medical stores and laboratories. Three other casualty clearing stations and a stationary hospital were detailed to deal with gas, ophthalmic, dental, nose ear and throat, venereal and dysentery and N.Y.D. cases, and the sick in the back areas. Ten ambulance trains were provided.'

By early August greatly increased numbers of heavy artillery units were being brought into camouflaged battle positions. At this stage 'shoots' to register on targets were kept to a minimum in order to avoid alerting the Germans. The London gunners of 309 Siege Battery noted how, in early August,

> 'the trenches behind our Franvillers positions suddenly became crowded with troops - young English lads, most of them. Fresh to this part of the country, they picked, as we had done, handfuls of apples off the trees by the roadside, and found, as we had done, that they were cider apples, "no bon".'[7]

Enormously thorough preparations were undertaken to ensure veterinary care for animals, cages for prisoners of war and the means to deal with the examination, evacuation and feeding of civilians in captured territory. Considerable concentrations of tanks were made as were both the British and French numbers of aeroplanes. The allied

An 8' howitzer team pose for the photographers at Warloy Baillon, 5 August 1918.

total of aircraft in the Amiens area was 1,904 whilst the Germans in the same area could muster only 365 planes. In the final week before the battle began this superiority was instrumental in ensuring the German's ignorance of the concentration of British men and material facing them. Exceptional care was taken to conceal and disguise the arrival of fresh Canadian troops, in the area to the south of the Somme. The first overt step in the operations which culminated in the Battle of Amiens was the taking over by the Australian Corps of 7,000 yards of frontage from the French. Just before the Australian Corps' extension of the British position the 5th Australian Division undertook an operation south of Morlancourt on 29 July when two battalions of 8 Brigade advanced some five hundred yards across a 2,000 yard frontage capturing 3 officers, 135 other ranks, two trench mortars and 36 machine guns. The consequential German reply was not forthcoming until 6 August, the delay creating a most difficult moment for the impending British offensive.

The 18th Division's history[8] describes the tense circumstances of these events well.

> 'Never had the Division participated in a battle which was kept so secret. The general plan was communicated to brigade and battalion commanders on 3rd August, and it was emphasised that only certain officers should be informed; no other officers, N.C.O.s, or men were to be allowed to learn the date and scope of the operation. In this respect the artillery had a particularly difficult task. By the night of 7th August 600 rounds per 18-pdr., and 500 rounds per 4.5 howitzer, had been conveyed to the

positions from which the batteries would open fire on the morning of 8th August. As these positions were in view of the enemy, there was no preliminary digging of gun-pits, no earth was allowed to be upturned; reconnaissance had to be reduced to a minimum; the guns themselves were not to be moved up until the night of the 7th. Also the thousands of rounds of ammunition had to be taken up under cover of darkness; and sorted and stacked, and hidden beneath hedges, under banks, among the uncut cornfields. The roads through Mericourt and Heilly on the night of 3rd August offered an unforgettable spectacle; hour after hour, through blinding torrents of rain, there moved an unending stream of ammunition wagons. For three nights these astounding processions continued. But in spite of them - in spite even of the Boche surprise attack of 6th August - the great secret did not leak out.

On a still night the creaking of the wheels of ammunition wagons can be heard a mile away. So still further to deceive the enemy, wheel tyres were lapped with rope, leather washers muffled the play of wheels, along parts of the Bray - Corbie road straw was laid, as in towns it is laid outside houses where the seriously ill are lying. The tanks, which also are noisy movers, were not brought into the area until the very eve of the battle.

Preparations for the attack were practically complete; General Lee and his staff were satisfied that nothing which should be done had been left undone. The sharp bursts of fire that on three mornings the enemy had put down on our front line, suggested that he was apprehensive and nervy; confidence that the Division was about to give a notably good account of itself grew stronger and stronger. Then suddenly on 6th August came perturbation, if not dismay. The Boche made a swift violent attack, and penetrated a thousand yards behind the line which the Division held astride the Bray-Corbie road.' (Map - Tour 3b & Walk 1)

The events of 6 August came as a complete surprise to the troops within the British III Corps. That morning they were engaged on the divisional reliefs consequential upon the extension of the III Corps' frontage down to the banks of the River Somme, the Australian Corps having been moved to their battle positions south of the river and towards Villers Bretonneux. In the area between Morlancourt and Sailly Laurette[9] the 18th and 58th Divisions were 'side slipping' to the south when, soon after dawn they were attacked by the newly re-equipped and well rested troops of the German 27th (Wurttemberg) Division. This German counter attack was a response to the Australian

During the early days of August patrols pushed deep into Albert, even though the fighting to capture the town would not commence until the third week of that month. Here a British sniper is seen operating amongst the wreckage on 6 August 1918.

advances of 29 July and was designed to re-exert German control over the higher ground south of Morlancourt which would give good observation over the River Somme. In the confusion and chaos the British lost a depth of 800 yards across a 4,000 yard width of frontage as well as losing more than 230 prisoners. Fortunately none of those prisoners revealed anything of the impending attack. It is worth noting that the high ground in question is marked by the prominent Beacon Cemetery from which all this terrain can be seen clearly.

The 6th August also marked the issue of final orders from General Debeney to the French First Army troops which would be attacking to the south of Fourth Army. His words set the tone for the sort of incisive and fluent advance which it was anticipated this massive joint assault would achieve.

> *'The attacks will be conducted with but one pre-occupation: to achieve the greatest rapidity in a succession of forward bounds. Once the front is broken, the divisions must march against their objectives, in the prescribed direction. Once an objective is captured, the attack against the next must be undertaken without delay.* Points d'appui[10] *will be taken by envelopment. Alignment is not to be sought; it is forbidden to wait for neighbouring divisions: liaison will be established by small detachments drawn from divisions in the second line.*

*The attacks will be pushed on and continued until night; from
the very first day the troops must go very far."* [11]

At 4.40 am on the 7th many of the British heavy artillery units had
begun to fire a long 'shoot' which then continued throughout the day
and subsequent night. 309 Siege Battery's men were in the thick of this
firing from their position outside Franvillers.

> *'Many men climbed the ridge on our right, and could see from
> there the effects of our firing - the steady bursts of the shells just
> beyond Morlancourt. It was not till the very end of this day that
> we had the first intimation that the great attack was just about to
> be launched, for at midnight the order suddenly came through
> for twenty gas-shells to be fused on each gun.'* [12]

In our area the night of 7-8 August saw the troops of III Corps in a state
of high tension. Fortunately the German army facing the Australians
and Canadians suspected nothing of that which was about to fall upon
them. Little interference with the final British preparations was made
by either German patrols or artillery other than the persistent gas
shelling of the Ancre valley floor. North of the River Somme, on the
right of Fourth Army's British troops, were the 58th Division. The front
lines here lay between Sailly Laurette in German hands and Sailly le
Sec behind the British positions. On the right of 58 Division and south
of the river, but outside the scope of this guide, were the Australian
Corps whose troops were also part of Fourth Army. On the left of the
58th Division stood the 18th Division which faced towards Gressaire
Wood, just north of the Chipilly spur, and Etinehem. Left and north of
the 18th Division were the 12th Division, which faced Morlancourt,

Fourth Army positions. 7/8 August 1918.

whilst on their left stood the 47th Division, facing Dernancourt and Meaulte. The role of the 47th Division was not to engage in the advance to be undertaken but rather to engage German troops in the Meaulte - Albert areas and thereby prevent interference with planned advances by the 58th and 18th Divisions towards Chipilly and Etinehem.

On 8th August 456 tanks were due to take part in the operations undertaken by Fourth Army. Of those, 96 were the light Whippet tanks.

The darkness was complete throughout a moonless but fine night. Towards 3.00 am a ground mist began to form within the valleys, gradually thickening to spread across the plateau (south of the Somme) which would see the main offensive launched, astride the Amiens - Foucaucourt road, east of Villers Brettoneux, by the Australian and Canadian Corps. Before zero, timed for 4.20 am, more than 430 tanks manoeuvred in order to be ready to advance with those infantry corps. North of the Somme the task of III Corps would be to protect the Australian's left flank and to secure the higher ground, overlooking the Somme's meandering and sluggish reed-beds, towards the twin villages of Cerisy and Chipilly. The stillness and moisture in the air was ideal for the German gunners who took full advantage to smother the Ancre valley and the Bray - Corbie road on the Morlancourt ridge with gas. Throughout it all, wondering whether the secrecy of the preparations had been compromised by the prisoners captured on the 6th, British troops waited in silent and tense anticipation.

1. The treaty of Brest-Litovsk, made between Russia and the Central Powers, had been signed on 3 March, 1918.
2. Franco-British conference on the unity of command, Doullens, 26 March, 1918.
3. PRO WO/95 2743. 47th Divisional Headquarters' Diary.
4. *Official History*, 1918 Vol 4. pp 38.
5. *The 18th Division in the Great War*, G.H.F.Nichols, William Blackwood & Sons, Edinburgh and London, 1922.
6. Fourth Army's order of battle was:
    III Corps.
        12th Division (35, 36, 37 Brigades).
        18th Division (53, 54, 55 Brigades).
        47th Division (140, 141, 142 Brigades).
        58th Division (173, 174, 175 Brigades).
        63rd Division (GHQ Reserve). American 33rd (Illinois) Division.
        74th Division came from XI Corps on 1/2nd September.
    Canadian Corps.
    Australian Corps.
    IX Corps
7. *London Gunners*. Kingham. Methuen & Co. Ltd. 1919.
8. *The 18th Division in the Great War*, Nichols, Blackwood and Sons, 1922. pp 337-8
9. 'Sailly Lorette' in the Official History Maps.
10. 'Points d'appui'. Translates literally as 'Support positions or points'.
11. *Official History*, 1918 Vol 4. pp 33-34
12. *London Gunners*. Kingham. Methuen & Co.Ltd. 1919.

Chapter Three

THE BRITISH (IMPERIAL) TROOPS' SECTOR OF THE BATTLE OF AMIENS
(8th-11th August)

This chapter, and the following, are enormously diverse in scope. Unlike comparable chapters in relatively small area/village guides such as *Thiepval* or *Guillemont* these pages cover a location which is dozens of square miles in extent. It is therefore impossible to detail the smallest units and personal experience in the way which characterises books dealing with single villages.

As we have seen, the objectives which had been set for the 58th Division within III Corps during the first day were to advance past Malard Wood and the southern tip of Gressaire Wood towards the great meander in the Somme which lay west and north-west of the village of Mericourt-sur-Somme. That advance would take the British infantry past strongly fortified positions on the Chipilly spur. Further north the 18th Division would capture the higher ground on the Morlancourt ridge before establishing a defensive front, facing north, to the south of Morlancourt. Beyond the 18th Division there was to be a minimal advance of the 12th Division, leaving Morlancourt to be pinched out the following day, 9 August.

South of the River Somme the Canadians and Australians, backed by huge numbers of tanks, made substantial gains, advances averaging more than five miles towards Foucaucourt and in the direction of Roye. One post war chronicler of the war described these events in stark brevity by saying that;

The broad and marshy valley floor of the River Somme today, seen here looking eastwards towards Chipilly from near to Corbie.

The magnificent architecture which marks the entrance to the Australian memorial at Villers Bretonneux.

> '...It was half past four on a misty morning when the enemy's advanced line heard the sudden crash of the gun-fire, and a moment later saw the monstrous forms of the tanks looming up through the grey light of dawn. Behind the tanks came the grim war-worn infantry. Everything went down before that united rush. The battle was won as soon as begun...'[1]

However, such pithiness does nothing to help navigation on the battlefield today! If you want to look out over the Australian sector of Fourth Army's battlefield on 8th August 1918 then the elevated central tower of the Australian memorial, found on the D23 road between Corbie and Villers Bretonneux, gives a particularly fine view of the southern locations described within this guide. Not far away, at Le Hamel, another large Australian memorial gives equally impressive views over the southern aspect of the Morlancourt ridge. That memorial was unveiled on 4th July 1998. The site includes useful explanations and has toilet facilities.

However, north of the River Somme the situation was rather different, due to two significant factors:

The central tower from which superb views can be had along the Somme valley and across the Morlancourt Ridge.

The village of Morlancourt within its deep cut valleys today.

Firstly, the terrain.

• The village of Morlancourt is surrounded by many deep valleys cut into the surrounding Morlancourt ridge. These valleys formed ideal locations within which the Germans found it possible to assemble reserves without being observed.

• The Morlancourt ridge between the River Somme and the River Ancre is a vast, open and exposed area of upland, which formed an ideal situation upon which German machine guns, each with substantial and interlocking fields of fire, could be deployed in defence. The lack of shelter available to attacking British troops would ensure heavy casualties when attacks were made from the most exposed positions. Running southwards, down towards the Somme, were the succession of parallel and deep ravines within which small woodlands provided further shelter for the German defenders. *(Maps - Tour 3b & 3c)*

Looking north-west across the confines of le Brache into Malard Wood and the Bois de Celestins. This location is typical of those steep valleys cut into the southern part of the Morlancourt plateau. This woodland was attacked and captured by the 6th Londons after the German's front positions had been overrun by the 6th and 7th Londons' soldiers of the 58th Division on 8 August 1918.

• The village of Chipilly provided admirable and secure observation for the German artillery, westwards up the course of the Somme valley and across much of the southern part of the Morlancourt ridge. *(Map - Walk 2)*

• The steep western descents into the many ravines, in some cases almost cliff like in their severity, provided a natural difficulty to attacking units. In descending these positions any infantry, mounted troops or mechanised vehicles would be exposed to fire from above and to the east. Simultaneously the same features in each subsequent valley to the east provided admirable positions within which to camouflage and deploy field guns and observation teams. In view of these difficulties no cavalry units and just one tank battalion, the 10th, had been allocated to III Corps on 8 August. From that tank battalion C Company was sent to the 58th Division on the banks of the Somme whilst A and B Companies were sent to the 18th Division which would attack across the open, almost plateau like, terrain south of Morlancourt.

Secondly, the Soldiers

• There was great concern that the British soldiers serving within III Corps were tired. These men had been in the line or close reserve throughout the first eight months of 1918, suffering heavily during the German March offensive. The 58th Division had also been engaged during the Battle of Villers Bretonneux on 24-25 April and had lost more than 3,500 all ranks. There was therefore a great shortage of experienced officers and NCOs and the ranks had been filled with many young soldiers. Testimony to the losses amongst these men of 18 of 1918 lie in profuse numbers in the cemeteries east of the Morlancourt plateau above Bray and towards the Canal du Nord.

• The confusion of many recent changes had eroded morale amongst III Corps' men who had been ordered to take over more frontage. In fact this had been done to facilitate the attacks to the south planned by the Australians and Canadians, but the men believed that it was a move made in response to poor French performance during the Second Battle of the Marne. This was taken as a bad omen since it mirrored the unfortunate extension of British lines near to St.Quentin before March 1918. Morale had taken a further battering on 6th August when the German 27th (Wurttemberg) Division had recaptured ground south west of Morlancourt. This had created localised difficulties in terms of the jumping off trenches and barrage plans. III Corps' staff were also under great organisational pressure since 54 Brigade (18th Division) was substituted, immediately prior to the assault on 8th August, by 36 Brigade (12th Division) because of casualties incurred during the Wurttemberger's attack on 6th August. From reserve the American 33rd Division (less 131st Regiment which went to 58th Division) was placed under the command of the 47th (London) Division. There was no British superiority in terms of troop numbers here - the four British divisions being faced by the equivalent of four German divisions[2].

Day one. The events of 8 August.

As the clock ticked away in the final hours before dawn the German artillery had been much more active here north of the River Somme than it was to the south. An enormous quantity of gas had been fired into the Ancre valley around Dernancourt on the north side of the Morlancourt plateau as well as into Heilly and Mericourt l'Abbe, behind the British front lines, where a great deal of troop movement was being undertaken. *(Map - Tour 2b)* In both Heilly and Mericourt l'Abbe the soldiers of 36 Brigade were caught in the gas as they marched up to relieve the battered 54 Brigade's men. All the combatants in the Ancre valley were forced to wear their respirators throughout the night and for many hours after the attack began because so much gas was trapped in the long grasses and crops which prevailed in the low lying valley areas. Above them, to the east, all across the Morlancourt plateau the Wurttembergers were well prepared, anticipating an attempt by the British to recover the ground lost on 6th August.

The consequences of the gas shelling and the enforced wearing of respirators meant that many units arrived at their jumping off trenches only minutes before zero. This was an especially serious problem for 36 Brigade's men (lent to the 18th Division from the 12th because of casualties amongst 54 Brigade) who knew nothing of the ground across which they were to attack. The combination of gas and mist meant that the few supporting tanks were delayed - none advancing with the first waves of infantry but later a number were involved in the mopping up operations. Fortunately the British artillery had a marked superiority in this area which enabled counter battery fire to prevent the withdrawal of many German artillery units. The advance was begun promptly at 4.20 am and within minutes it became apparent that the war was reaching towards a decisive moment. Torrents of German prisoners were taken as their front lines were completely overrun. I have taken the three division's assaults in sequence from the right, on the banks of the Somme, to the left of III Corps. Perhaps the best vantage point from which to visualise the events described here is the site of Beacon Cemetery on the D1 Corbie - Bray road.

The 58th (2/1st London) Division.

Soon after zero the village of Sailly Laurette was captured by the 2/10 Londons (175 Brigade) who surprised the village's garrison by the speed of their advance. By 6.30 am only two machine guns hidden in the wreckage of the church were still holding out, and those were dealt with by one of the two tanks allotted to this battalion. Three hours later the 2/10th Londons were one thousand yards east of Sailly Laurette on the ridge between the village and Malard Wood, the Germans having fallen back to that wood and the adjacent Bois de Celestins. In the fighting for this commanding position the Londons had captured an arsenal of weaponry including 98 machine guns and 23 trench mortars as well as 285 prisoners! From here the London's machine gunners were able to train their guns on Chipilly village, 2,500 yards to the east. *(Maps - Walk 1 & Walk 2)*

North of the 2/10 Londons the advance was made by 174 Brigade who employed the 6th and 7th Londons in the front with the 8th Londons in reserve. The advance of these units saw the eastern perimeter of Malard Wood captured by 8.00 am, although small groups

Looking east along the Morlancourt Ridge past the villages of Sailly-le-Sec and Sailly Laurette, along the course of the River Somme, towards the village of Chipilly. The slopes above Sailly Laurette were captured by the 2/10th Londons on the morning of 8 August whilst the 3rd Australian Division advanced on the right of the river.

Looking south, across the River Somme's valley, towards le Hamel and the scene of the 3rd Australian Division's advance.

of Germans persisted within its confines until the early afternoon.

Unfortunately the final objectives could not be reached by the 58th Division and 173 Brigade was detailed to effect this final part of the advance. Following closely behind the soldiers of 174 Brigade 173's men had also passed through Malard Wood. As soon as the two assault battalions of 173 Brigade, the 3rd and 2/4th Londons, left the shelter of Malard Wood they had been subject to heavy and accurate machine gun fire from the slopes north of Chipilly, only a small number of men advancing further east towards the higher ground on the Chipilly ridge. Belief that some British troops were holding Chipilly ridge caused much delay throughout the day. This was a real problem for the Australians on the south of the Somme who were taking many casualties from machine guns, in the village of Chipilly, firing in enfilade. Therefore the 2/2nd Londons were brought up from brigade reserve. After an initial delay, consequential upon concerns about the whereabouts of the most advanced British troops, the 2/2nd Londons advanced at 3.00 pm only to be met by a hail of machine gun fire from the front as well as from the north around Gressaire Wood and the south-east from the slopes above Chipilly. The battalion was forced to fall back into the shelter of Malard Wood. *(See Map overleaf)*

Later that evening, at 7.30 pm, a further attempt to advance to the eastern side of the Chipilly spur was made by 175 Brigade and with the co-operation of 2/10th Londons who would advance from Sailly Laurette. However it was again very clear that the overwhelming strength of the German machine gun positions on the west facing slopes of the spur north of the village of Chipilly would prevent any advance. Some small groups from the 2/2nd Londons did get as far as the Morlancourt road, north of Chipilly overlooking the valley, but were under such pressure that they were withdrawn at midnight.

The 18th (Eastern) Division.

This was to feature an extraordinary assault by the soldiers of 36 Brigade (who had been sent from the 12th Division to support the 18th Division following the German surprise attacks on 6th August in the area of Beacon cemetery). Having been gassed on the way up and having been forced to wear respirators throughout that march, they had arrived at unfamiliar jumping off trenches knowing nothing of the ground across which they were to attack - apart from scanty information gleaned from 1:40,000 maps available to their officers. The attack was made by the 7th Royal Sussex and 9th Royal Fusiliers and succeeded in recapturing the ground lost to the Wurttembergers on 6th August. However, in spite of losing twenty officers and some 500 men, these two battalions were unable to progress past their first objective, the road running between Morlancourt and Malard Wood. That task was completed at great cost by the 10th Essex, 53 Brigade. The survivors, numbering perhaps 80, of whom many were mere youths, under the command of Lieutenant Colonel T.M.Banks and Major Forbes, then began to move eastwards, their advance astride the Bray - Corbie road shrouded in mist. This band of men advanced some 2,500 yards to the northern continuation of Gressaire Wood where they

Taken from *The 18th Division in the Great War* pp 355, showing the planned objectives of the 18th Division's soldiers during the initial fighting on the Morlancourt ridge, 8th August 1918.

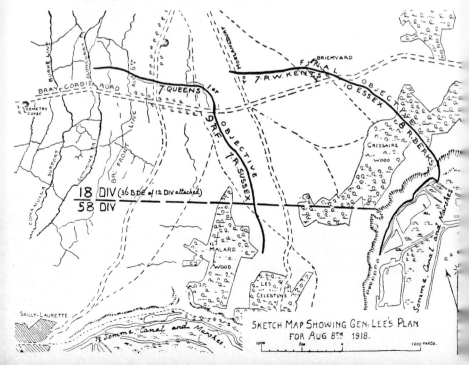

SKETCH MAP SHOWING GEN: LEE'S PLAN FOR AUG 8TH 1918.

surprised and captured two 4-gun batteries of field artillery. Confident that their final objectives had been reached Banks' men began to dig in by 7.20 am. By 7.50 the very much depleted West Kents, with the assistance of two tanks, arrived at the brickyard (la Briqueterie) on the Bray - Corbie road to link with the 10th Essex. Unfortunately, on their right, the bulk of Gressaire Wood was still held by a German reserve battalion and Banks' party's right flank was unsupported. Within a few minutes the situation in this area became serious for the 7th West Kents and the 10th Essex. On their right a field gun opened fire on their position from a range of 500 yards whilst from the north a German infantry force from Morlancourt was attacking the tiny numbers of the West Kents whose men were strung out along some 2,500 yards of frontage. To the south of Banks' force the 8th Royal Berkshires were unable to get into the southern part of Gressaire Wood in the face of heavy machine gun and field artillery fire. By 9.00 am the Berks' survivors were forced to concede ground and pull back to their first objectives. The 10th Essex were thus in danger of being enveloped from their right as well as having any retreat cut off by the attacks on the 7th West Kents. When the anticipated German counter attack from Gressaire Wood was launched the 10th Essex were compelled to retreat, eventually falling back to the old British trenches which had been their first objectives. The 10th Essex were at this stage reduced to a party no more than 15 strong.

To the north of 36 Brigade the attack was carried out by 55 Brigade's 7th Queen's. Their task was to seize the ground on the north of the Bray - Corbie road. This battalion faced a resilient counter attack by German soldiers belonging to the 120th and 123rd regiments of the 27th Division. Not waiting to be attacked through the mist in their own trenches the Germans had swept forward behind a shower of stick

The remains of the Brickyard, on the Bray - Corbie road, are still clearly visible today. The brickyard site can be easily located using the IGN 1;25000 series 2408 Albert ouest which covers all of the Morlancourt ridge area. Travel east for 2.5 kilometres from Beacon Cemetery and the site of the brickyard lies overgrown with grass on the left of the Bray road at a junction with a lane leading back to Morlancourt on the left. *(See map opposite)*

grenades, causing the 7th Queen's to lose their barrage and become engaged in close quarter fighting in the area of Cloncurry trench, a part of the line which the 18th Division had lost on 6th August. Within a short time isolated parties of the Queen's were being overrun and it was left to their commanding officer, Lieutenant Colonel Christopher Bushell, V.C., D.S.O., to bring forwards the remaining details at 7.00 am and drive the Germans back from the old British front line. Whilst directing the tanks, which were now making their way forward, and exhorting his men Bushell was shot through the neck and mortally wounded. Bushell is buried at Querrieu British Cemetery, south-west of Albert on the road towards Amiens.

Cloncurry trench, an old British support position, lay almost directly opposite the site of Beacon Cemetery. The actual British front lines which had existed in this area and been lost in the German attacks of 6th August were located a little way to the east of Beacon Cemetery and lay some 300 metres west of the D42 Sailly Laurette - Morlancourt road as it crosses the Morlancourt ridge. That slightly higher ground between Beacon Cemetery and the road was surmounted, before the war, by a brick beacon clearly marked on contemporary trench maps (reference 20,a,5,4). Even today it is immediately clear why this position was a vital one to recapture, prior to any subsequent advances eastwards along the Morlancourt ridge, since the location provided dominant observation in this area.

The attack of the 18th Division therefore ended on their first objectives, although their advance could have seen the capture of Gressaire Wood with more good fortune and a better performance from the tanks. Many of the tanks had lost direction in the morning mist. The official history reports, rather half-heartedly, that:

'*Of one company four tanks broke down before arrival at their starting point. Of the second company, four were held in reserve, one lost direction and joined the 12th Division, and two broke down. The others are said to have engaged any machine gun posts which could be located. The reserve section went as far as the second objective. Seventeen of the 36 tanks rallied in the evening.*'[3]

Taken from *The 18th Division in the Great War* pp284 Lieutenant Colonel Christopher Bushell, V.C., D.S.O., M.C. Bushell had won the V.C. on 23rd March and had only just recovered from the wounds which he had incurred on that occasion.

The casualties amongst the infantry battalions involved here were high, 290 among the 10th Essex, 256 among the 7th Queens, 166 among the Berkshires and 192 among the West Kents. Although not a complete success these events had, by virtue of commanding the Morlancourt ridge, secured the left flank of Fourth Army's advance.

The 12th Division.

On the left flank of III Corps, the attacks made by the 12th Division immediately south of the Ancre were a subsidiary to the main events on the Morlancourt ridge involving the 18th and 58th Divisions. The tactical circumstances of the 12th Division's men had been improved by the fact that the Germans had already begun, in the days prior to 8th August, to withdraw from Dernancourt and other positions on the western bank of the Ancre. Nevertheless, the heavy gas shelling of the Ancre valley during the night 7/8th claimed one notable casualty when Brigadier General Vincent, commanding 35 Brigade, was temporarily replaced by Br.General Beckwith. The morning dawned shrouded in a dense mist in the Ancre valley which was added to by the effect of smoke shells whose purpose was to help give direction to the young soldier's advance. The 12th Division's attack, carried out by 35 Brigade, achieved great success, an advance of almost 1,000 yards towards Morlancourt from just east of Ville-sur-Ancre being made. *(Maps 2a & Tour 3c)* This attack was launched two hours after zero at 6.20 am and was undertaken by half the 1/1st Cambridge on the right, adjacent to the 18th Division's men, with the 7th Norfolks and 9th Essex to their left. The advance was initially checked by a counter attack on the Cambridge men which drove those men to their starting lines. During this time the German machine gunners on the Sailly Laurette to Morlancourt road were holding the combined advance of both the 18th Division and 35 Brigade of the 12th Division. The Cambridge battalion's two support companies were then brought up to enable the final advance to be undertaken at 12.25. Throughout these events more than 600 prisoners were taken. Towards evening a large German force was seen approaching along the road east of Morlancourt but this concentration of troops was scattered by the artillery fire of the 18th Division's guns as well as the 12th Division's machine gun battalion.

During 8 August Fourth Army had captured 13,000 prisoners and over 300 guns. Further south the French First Army captured 3,350 prisoners. This was the beginning of the end of German resistance. Subsequent events on the old 1916 Somme battlefield confirmed this

This photograph shows a captured German 77mm field gun being made ready for removal from the Malard Wood area.

weakening of the German defence as the British Army pressed home its advantage. That, however, is not to imply that German resistance had already collapsed. Events about to unfold during the following three months marked a savage period of conflict during which casualties, amongst British infantry units engaged, rose to some of their highest levels recorded during the war.

Day two. The events of 9 August.

Thus, at the end of 8 August, a secure position had been established overlooking Morlancourt whilst, further south, the ground lost on 6 August had been recaptured and Sailly Laurette and Malard Wood brought into the control of British hands. The plans to capitalise on this situation the following day were necessarily complex.

• American 131st Regiment (part of the 33rd American Division) to be attached to 58th Division.

• 58th Division, to the south, and 12th Division (to the north) to attack at dawn on 9 August and to incorporate the frontage then held by the 18th Division. The 12th Division would pinch out Morlancourt and pass on to the old Amiens Outer Defence Lines which ran from Dernancourt in the direction of Etinehem. The 58th would advance past Gressaire Wood in order to facilitate the capture of the Chipilly spur. 174 Brigade with the support of three tanks was to occupy Chipilly and the ridge above it. 173 Brigade was to side slip south to make room for the American 131st Regiment which would attack Gressaire Wood with five tanks belonging to the 10th Tank Battalion. 175 Brigade would form the left wing of this attack.

The village of Chipilly and its spur above the Somme had been well known to the 1916 Tommies, many of whom had become familiar with these slopes during training for their part in 30th Division's assaults on Montauban on 1 July of that year. Chipilly dominates its sister village, Cerisy, on the south bank of the Somme, as well as the western approaches along the marshy bed of that river. North-east of Chipilly the high ground at the top of the spur commands much of the southern part of the Morlancourt ridge. The Chipilly spur was well protected by a shallow ravine, marked as 'Petite Vallee' on IGN maps, running north from the village towards Gressaire Wood. The remaining steeply sloping sides of the spur are surrounded by the River Somme making infantry approaches treacherously difficult. The importance of the location had not been lost on another General, Julius Caesar, whose legionnaires had, during their campaign to subjugate Gaul to Rome, constructed an encampment here whose embankments are still visible today. The valley north of Chipilly was protected by machine guns firing across it from within Gressaire Wood. To make matters more difficult the Germans had constructed a series of concrete machine gun positions on both the west and east slopes of the spur, just beneath the highest ground. Finally, a number of field guns within deeply dug fortifications in the village commanded the river bridge which linked Chipilly to Cerisy as well as the road approaches from the west. This ground is mapped in Chapter 6, Tour 3.

The location of the Germans fortifications and machine gun emplacements along the high ground of the Chipilly spur.

The 58th Division.

The dawn attack was postponed due to the difficulty of assembling the troops. It was not until 4.15 pm that the 6th Londons of 174 Brigade, 58th Division, attacked Chipilly in the face of severe enfilade fire from Les Celestins[4] as well as from the ridge above Chipilly. In this attempt they were supported by the initiative of men belonging to the 2/10th Londons who had remained in the south east corner of Malard Wood overnight. The London's men then worked south-eastwards down the valley until they were forced to call for more artillery support to quell the machine gun fire from their emplacements on the terraces just below the summit of the Chipilly spur or ridge. Under the direction of two Australians who were already familiar with the approaches to Chipilly the 2/10th Londons then entered the village under the protection of a smokescreen fired by the artillery. These Australians then pushed around the south of the village, above the banks of the Somme, and then rushed the machine gun positions on the spur's summit. This attack was then supplemented by K Company of the 3rd Battalion of the American 131st Regiment, enabling a line to be secured, east of Chipilly and across the high ground north-east of the village, by 8.00 pm, allowing the soldiers of 173 Brigade to complete the capture of their objectives up to the south-eastern edge of Gressaire Wood.

By this time III Corps' main attack, launched at 5.30 pm, had already cost many casualties. The right arm of that attack was made from the eastern face of Malard Wood by the remnants of the 3rd, 2/4th and 2/2nd Londons (173 Brigade). However, when they reached the Morlancourt - Chipilly road, overlooking the valley north of Chipilly, the men were again held up by the intensity of machine gun fire coming from Gressaire Wood, and from Chipilly as well as the machine gun posts on the slopes north of the village. It was not until 8.00 pm that the soldiers of 173 Brigade were able to complete their advance after the 2/10th Londons had taken Chipilly village.

The centre of III Corps' attack was made by the Americans' 131st Regiment. There was great enthusiasm amongst these men whose position, just 90 minutes before the attack was due, was some three and half miles behind their assembly trenches. Marching as fast as humanly possible and running the last mile into Malard Wood from whence they deployed to face Gressaire Wood, the Americans were desperate to ensure that they did not miss the barrage. This attack was made by the 1st and 2nd Battalions in the front with the 3rd Battalion

Looking north across Petite Vallee into Gressaire Wood from the Chipilly spur. German machine gunners at this location enfiladed the attacks made by the American 131st Regiment moving left to right across the fields in front of Gressaire Wood on the skyline. *(Contemporary photograph superimposed on present day location.)*

in support. As they moved between Malard and Gressaire woods, less than a mile in distance, the men began to suffer heavy casualties from machine gun fire emanating from Gressaire Wood and also in enfilade from the machine gun emplacements below the summit of Chipilly ridge. The crossing of the open ground between the two woods took almost two hours and had to be supported by a company of the 3rd Battalion as well as by the 7th Londons. It is a measure of how under strength the British battalions were at this time that the 7th Londons attacked with 17 officers and just 360 other ranks, losing 14 of those officers and 300 other ranks as casualties this day. By 8.00 pm the Americans were able to take their left objectives in the south west corner of Gressaire Wood and a little later their objectives to the right of their attack, where they abutted to the soldiers of 173 Brigade.

The view east along the Bray - Corbie road from the high ground beyond Beacon Cemetery. This is the open ground across which 175 Brigade's men attacked on 9 August 1918. In the distance the woods on the left of the road are the Bois des Tailles whilst those on the right are Gressaire Wood.

175 Brigade was due to advance eastwards, at 5.30 pm, along the line of the Bray - Corbie road past the site of la Briqueterie to the valley running between Gressaire Wood, on the south of the road, and the Bois des Tailles to the north of the road. 175 Brigade would therefore capture Gressaire Wood in conjunction with the American 131st Regiment. This stretch of the Bray - Corbie road, the D1, is very flat and crosses open, utterly shelterless, fields. Prior to the attack the soldiers had been withdrawn from their front lines into the confines of the deep ravine between Sailly le Sec and Sailly Laurette. The 8th Londons were attached to 175 Brigade for the purposes of this attack. It was the 12th and 8th Londons who made the assault, supported by the 5th Royal Berkshires with the 9th Londons detailed to maintain touch with the American 131st Regiment's attack on the southern aspect of Gressaire Wood. By 8.00 pm the bulk of 175 Brigade's objectives had been achieved and it was soon discovered that Gressaire Wood held a remarkable collection of artillery pieces: 70 guns and howitzers being found including 8', 5.9', 4.2', 4.1' and 3.7' calibre pieces.

Throughout the rest of the daylight hours the 131st Regiment and the 58th Division's men pushed patrols forward in the direction of the previously British occupied Amiens Outer Line, which ran along the eastern sides of Gressaire Wood and the Bois des Tailles towards Dernancourt. This old position, used in the spring of 1917 before the German retirement to the Hindenburg positions, was in some places a three mile wide desolation of trenches, barbed wire and interlocking shell-holes which provided an ideal warren within which German machine gunners could operate. Therefore German rearguard actions were able to prevent British troops from occupying those positions immediately but it was becoming clear that, north of the Somme, the Germans were retiring to their old early 1917 positions, parallel to the British Amiens Outer Line, known as the Etinehem - Meaulte positions.

The 12th Division.

The capture of Morlancourt by the 12th Division was to be undertaken by 37 Brigade. Initially the attack was planned for first light, 4.30 am, but was postponed in order to bring it into line with the attacks to be made further south by the 58th Division. Unfortunately those orders failed to reach the 6th Buffs in time and that battalion advanced across the south of Morlancourt with little difficulty. The battalion was soon recalled and came back with a prisoner, ten trench mortars, a machine gun and very few casualties! *(Map - Tour 3c)*

The actual attack, when it came at 5.30 pm, was to cost many more casualties. Punctually the 6th Buffs advanced again across the southern aspect of the village, and at 6.20 pm the 6th Queen's moved against the northern aspect of the village. After being outflanked Morlancourt would be cleared later by the 1/1st Cambridgeshires. Both battalions were protected by an impressive creeping artillery barrage and a number of tanks but faced stiff opposition from well sited machine gun posts within the village as well as a field gun firing over open sights. Privates K.Caldwell and R.H.Wallace of the 6th Buffs were able to overcome the gun's crew by Lewis gun fire enabling their comrades to advance. To the north of the Queen's the 6th Royal West Kents advanced quickly, inspired initially by the sight of their battalion commander, the flamboyant and brave Lieutenant Colonel Dawson, leading his men into action on horseback! Dawson's soldiers were able to reach the old Amiens Outer Defence Lines south-east of Dernancourt. During this advance by the Royal West Kents a further fifteen machine guns and four trench mortars were captured. This was the action which saw the winning of a Victoria Cross by Sergeant Thomas James Harris, of the West Kents. The citation was published in the London Gazette, 2 Oct.1918.

'*Thomas James Harris, Sergt., No. 358, M.M., late Royal West Kent Regt. Lower Hailing, Kent. For most conspicuous bravery and devotion to duty in attack when the advance was much impeded by hostile machine guns concealed in crops and shell-holes. Sergt. Harris led his section against one of these, capturing it and killing seven of the enemy. Later, on two successive occasions, he attacked single-handed two enemy machine guns - which were causing heavy casualties and holding up the advance. He captured the first gun and killed the crew, but was himself killed when attacking the second one. It was largely due to the great courage and initiative of this gallant N.C.O. that the advance of the battalion was continued without delay and undue casualties. Throughout the operations he showed a total disregard for his own personal safety, and set a magnificent example to all ranks.*'

Sergeant Thomas James Harris, V.C., M.M. Killed in Action, 9th August 1918. Sergeant Harris is buried within Dernancourt Communal Cemetery Extension.

The clearance of Morlancourt village was achieved by the 1/1st Cambridgeshires who were attached to 37 Brigade. Without waiting for tank support the Cambridgeshires had advanced at 5.30 pm and swept through the village incurring the loss of only two officers and 10 other ranks. Again a huge booty of machine guns, nineteen in all, as well as trench mortars were captured. There is an interesting reference within the Official History to a Company Sergeant Major Betts (later killed on 22nd August), 'who single-handed worked his way to the rear of the defenders, and opened fire on them.' The 12th Division's history says that one of his actions was 'to capture, single handed, a nest of four machine guns and thirty men'. It is most unusual for any non commissioned officer to be mentioned in this way unless in the recording of an act which led to the award of the Victoria Cross. Betts' actions were clearly instrumental in the capture of Morlancourt.

47th Division.

In a minor action north of the River Ancre the capture of Dernancourt was secured this day, by the 47th Division's men, marking the northernmost action during the Battle of Amiens. By this time the exposed westernmost parts of the town of Albert had been evacuated by German troops, although the bulk of the town and its cellars east of the Ancre were still strongly held

The capture of Morlancourt and Dernancourt mark the end of the second day's fighting during the Battle of Amiens within the area covered by this guide. Across the battlefield as a whole Fourth Army had now captured 387 German officers as well as 15,516 of their other ranks. The French effort towards Montdidier had netted 150 officers and 4,300 other ranks. But there was a sense that attacks had not achieved all that could have been done. Many attacks north of the Somme were not co-ordinated with timings to the south. Too many attacks were postponed. Some units advanced unsupported. There were too many examples of what is often the outcome of delay - 'Order, counter order, disorder.'!

Day three. The events of 10 August.

This day saw a substantial change in the organisation of Fourth Army units. The River Somme had not proved to be a good boundary between the Australian Corps and III Corps and it was decided to make the Bray - Corbie road into that boundary. This decision explains why the 3rd Australian Division's memorial is sited at the cross roads where the Sailly-le-Sec to Mericourt l'Abbe road crosses the D1. The consequences were that:

- The 3rd Australian Division took over the 58th Division's sector.
- The 58th Division left the sector to rest and refit. The 18th Division was brought back into the front line.
- The bulk of the American 33rd Division was transferred to the Australian Corps.
- The 47th (2nd London) Division from the Albert sector was made into III Corps' reserve.

Therefore little could be done on this day to capitalise upon the capture of Morlancourt and the arrival of British troops in the old Amiens Defence Lines. What was done north of the Somme on 10 August can be divided into three separate actions, summarised thus:

- The village of Etinehem, south-east of Gressaire Wood on the banks of the Somme, was captured by the Australian 13 Brigade, who then advanced in the direction of Bray-sur-Somme.
- Still acting under the orders of the 58th Division the 1st and 2nd Battalions of the American 131st Regiment pressed forward during the night 9-10 August to the east of the Bois des Tailles and across the ravine on the east side of that woodland. The old

Looking north into the valley east of the Bois des Tailles which was crossed by the 1st and 2nd Battalions of the American 131st Regiment on the morning of 10 August. On the top of the eastern slopes lay the old Amiens Outer Defence Lines which formed a formidable defensive position of which the German rearguards took full advantage. A short distance to the east is the village of Bray which, from 10th August, became the focus of the Australian advance which had now been expanded to include positions north of the Somme but south of the Bray - Corbie road.

Amiens Defence Lines were located on the top of the east side of that ravine and were occupied by the Americans by mid-day on 10 August.

During this day 175 Brigade, part of the 58th Division, was still operating in the area facing the north of Bois des Tailles. Brigadier General Maxwell-Scott's headquarters were within la Briqueterie, 1500 metres west of Bois des Tailles on the D1, identified on the 1:20,000 trench map 62d NE at K.16.c.9,5. The earthworks which surrounded the brickworks can still be seen today. Initial attacks by 175 Brigade's soldiers were driven from the ravine east of Bois des Tailles by concentrations of mustard gas and artillery fire. However, by 2.10 pm the 9th Londons achieved their objective on the east of that ravine and two support battalions, the 12th Londons and the 5th Berkshires, were sent forward to occupy the old Amiens Defence Lines as far north as the light railway which was at the junction between 58th and 12th Divisions operations. This railway line was the one which ran from Dernancourt up to Morlancourt and thence past the site of Grove Town cemetery, past the northern end of Happy  Valley and on to The Loop north of Bray-sur-Somme. The line had been used extensively during 1916 but was again reduced to wreckage by the fighting in the spring, summer and early autumn of 1918.

• In the 12th Division's area, south of Meaulte, the 6th Buffs, 9th Essex and the 6th Queen's together with six tanks of the 10th Battalion made their attack in line across the ridge's flat top at 6.00 pm. This assault succeeded in capturing some ground, but the Germans retained control of a knoll of greater elevation, Hill 105, lying 2,500 metres south of Meaulte and a similar distance east-north-east of Morlancourt, which is the highest point on this part of Morlancourt Ridge. *(Map - Tour 3c)*

The events of 10 August mark the end of serious fighting on the Morlancourt ridge, within the confines of this guide, during the first fortnight of August. Only on the 22nd was the assault recommenced in this area. It was unfortunate that Hill 105, which had been reached and

A Mark V tank, J18, belonging to 10th Tank Battalion, 9 August 1918, camouflaged from observation before their attacks south of Meaulte on 10 August.

cleared by the tanks, could not be held by the 6th Buffs, since this was an ideal location from which to observe across Meaulte towards Albert, the battle for which was already being planned. This day, 10 August, Haig issued orders to Third Army, in the Albert - Arras sector, instructing it to:

> 'carry out raids and minor operations in order to ascertain the enemy's intentions on the Albert - Arras front, and to take immediate advantage of any favourable situation which the main operations may create, and push advance guards in the general direction of Bapaume.'[5]

The casualty returns for this period make interesting reading and give the lie to the popular misconception that it was the Empire units of the

10 August, 1918. The elevated and open ground on the Chipilly spur provides little shelter from German artillery or the summer's heat. Here troops congregate around a collection post with many items of salvaged equipment.

Canadian and Australian Corps which invariably endured the greater part of the fighting on this front. During the period 7 - 15th August the total casualties within III Corps were higher than the Australian Corps to the right of III Corps!

	Officers			Other Ranks			
	K.	W.	M.	K.	W.	M.	Total
12th Div.	23	55	2	175	1,288	306	1,849
18th Div.	12	55	15	176	1,069	668	1,995
58th Div.	23	84	4	264	1,597	434	2,406
							6,250

During the period 8 - 13th August the five divisions of the Australian Corps suffered a total of 5,991 casualties[6]. I think it fair to conclude that the difficulties faced by the British troops on Morlancourt Ridge to the left of the Australians are all too often underestimated whilst the importance of the role played by the Australians on the opening three days of the Battle of Amiens is often overstated.[7]

1. *The British Campaign in France and Flanders. July to November 1918.* Doyle. Hodder and Stoughton.
2. One regiment of the 43rd Division.
One regiment of the 108th Division under command of 43rd Div. (The 108th was in the act of relieving the 43rd.)
The 27th Division together with an infantry and artillery regiment of the 26th Reserve Division.
The artillery of the resting 107th & 243rd Divisions.
The 54th Reserve Division.
The 233rd Division.
3. Official History. 1918 Vol 4, pp 80-81.
4. Today the Bois de Celestins is effectively an eastern continuation of Malard Wood.
5. Official History, 1918 Vol 4, pp 135.
6. Official History, 1918 Vol 4, pp 158-9.
7. Interestingly, after the war, many of III Corps' and especially the 58th Division's dead were removed from the original battlefield cemeteries, in the vicinity of their campaign, and reburied in Villers-Bretonneux cemetery.

Chapter Four

THE BATTLE OF ALBERT AND SUBSEQUENT EVENTS UNTIL EARLY SEPTEMBER

General Sir Julian Byng.

In the vicinity of Albert and north towards Arras the Third Army, commanded by General Sir Julian Byng, began operations on 21 August. This followed a considerable extension of the French attack the day before, 20 August. To the south of Third Army the Fourth Army, commanded by General Sir Henry Rawlinson, would continue to press home the advantage. On the north bank of the Somme, in support of the Third Army's right flank, the Fourth Army's attack would begin on 22 August, south of the Somme on 23 August. The first phase of Third Army's attack was a limited one

General Sir Henry Rawlinson.

with the objective of capturing the line of the Albert - Arras railway line. In the area of V Corps this line, familiar to the soldiers who had been here during the period 1915 to 1917, ran north-east from Albert along the western side of the River Ancre. The following day, 22 August, it was anticipated that the left flank of Fourth Army would be moved forward between the Somme and the Ancre. On 23 August the Third Army with the left flank of the Fourth Army would then deliver a full scale attack. This book's coverage extends to the northern limits of V Corps[1] operations within Third Army. That northern limit of V Corps is a line drawn from Beaumont Hamel to Warlencourt, thence south of Ligny Thilloy towards Lechelle and Ytres. Ytres is above the Canal du Nord some 16 kilometres north of Peronne and 12 kilometres east-south-east of Bapaume. The advance of V Corps therefore covers almost all of the British sector of the 1916 Somme battlefield. The divisions forming V Corps of Third Army were the 38th (Welsh), the 17th and the 21st, with the 33rd from II Corps on 18 August.

Contemporary statistics show that 50% of Third Army's soldiers were boys, often since described as the 'men of 18 of 1918'. It was believed that these men would do well if the first action which they took part in was a success. As had been the case at the Battle of Amiens, much emphasis was placed upon secrecy and no preliminary bombardments were to be fired until the moment of attack. For the main attack of IV and VI Corps zero was set for 4.55 am, but in V Corps' area zero was set fifty minutes later, at 5.45 am. The main thrust of V Corps' attack was anticipated as south-easterly, across the Ancre valley towards the Pozieres ridge.

There were a number of features to this fighting which unfolded in the coming two weeks which make its understanding different to the static events of 1915 - early 1917 in this area.

• The fact that battalions had an almost complete lack of training in conditions of open warfare. Such was these men's inexperience that their attacks would be led by artillery barrages containing a very high percentage of smoke shell, designed as much to guide these soldiers advance as to prepare their passage.

• The fitness and enthusiasm of the 18 and 19 year olds who formed a significant proportion of every British battalion. Although easily discouraged by adversity these soldiers had great vitality and powers of recuperation.

• The relative numerical weakness of the battalions by comparison with the complements which were available in 1916. Typically a 1918 battalion was 400 - 500 strong.

• The German defence did not make use of continuous seams of trenches - even though the British advance was conducted across terrain deeply scarred by thousands of miles of old entrenchments. German policy was to hold ground by means of fire in depth using a co-ordinated pattern of artillery and machine gun fire to inflict casualties and achieve defence.

• It was not possible to maintain continuous liaison between attacking infantry and their artillery. The accuracy of artillery fire was reduced in conditions of mobile warfare since the guns were constantly on the move. This was especially problematic for the heavier units who were often brought into action using hastily prepared positions and were not firing on pre-registered targets. Much field artillery fire was launched against map co-ordinates at the request of local brigade or even battalion commanders. From August 8th onwards even the 6' Siege Battery Brigades were attached to divisions rather than taking orders from Corps' headquarters which were unable to keep pace with the rapid unfolding of events. The outcome was that 'in future we were generally less than a mile from the front-line trenches, instead of being three or four miles behind, as previously. Being so advanced we were naturally able to do highly effective work on

Fritz's batteries, and in hindering his retreat. But from the personal point of view .... our splendid 6' guns seemed to be mere trench mortars, we almost felt that we had the dangers of the infantryman's life without the shelter of his trenches.'[2]

• Touch with the retreating German soldiers was frequently lost, but a steady forward momentum within the range of artillery support was then undertaken by advance guards, with mounted troops undertaking reconnaissance both in front and on the flanks. Throughout this period the overall intention was to press the German army eastwards without attempting any deep infiltration of his positions.

The events of 21 August.

This day, the first in the Battle of Albert, saw V Corps of Third Army engaged in the attempt to cross the River Ancre, a preliminary operation prior to the resumption of the Fourth Army's offensive the following day. The Corps' dispositions consisted of the 21st Division in the Grandcourt area, the 17th in the Hamel - St.Pierre Divion area, with the 38th Division on their right in the vicinity of Aveluy facing Thiepval Wood and Authuille. The experience of the 21st Division during the coming two weeks was as the northernmost unit within V Corps. The 38th now faced a difficult time in the swamp like vicinity of the Ancre which, ever since 1915, had been subjected to periods of intense artillery bombardment which had destroyed the embankments of the canalised sections above the valley floor proper. The resultant flooded marshland was a difficult natural obstacle, sometimes in excess of three hundred meters in width, made even more forbidding by the addition of great quantities of barbed wire and fallen trees.

The valley of the Ancre at the dual bridges east of the village of Aveluy, north of Albert. Here the canalised section of the river is distinguishable from the river course proper.

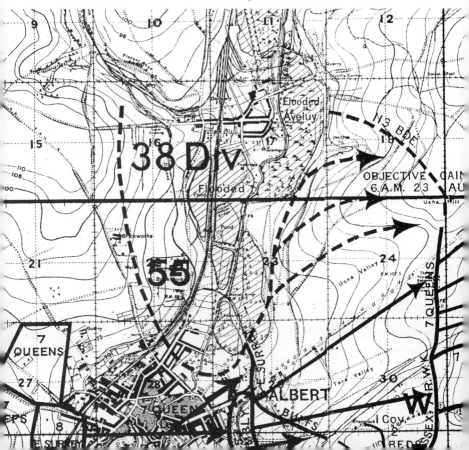

V Corps' task was to press forward to the River Ancre, across a frontage extending from just south of Aveluy to positions just north of Beaucourt. In the event of success the Corps was to extend that frontage, pushing across the Ancre between Hamel and Miraumont in a south-easterly direction and then, having threatened the Thiepval heights from the north, to cross the Ancre between Hamel and Albert moving past Authuille in the direction of Thiepval from the west.

At 5.45 am Beaucourt was attacked and captured by the 2nd Lincolnshires (62 Brigade, 21st Division). This attack cost very few

Taken from *The 18th Division in the Great War*, G.H.F.Nichols, this shows the area of the flooded Ancre valley north of Albert. (Squares W 27-30 and northwards to northern limit of map.)

Looking north-west across the Ancre valley from the Ulster Tower. To reveal Hamel, Beaumont Hamel and Beaucourt. This is the area attacked by 62 and 110 Brigades on the morning of 21 August 1918.

casualties and by 7.00 am the reserves of the 2nd Lincolns along with the 1st Lincolns were passing through the village as they advanced to capture the railway line on the north bank of the Ancre. Throughout these early hours the fighting took place in extensive mist which filled the valley floor.

South of Beaucourt, but north of St.Pierre Divion, the 12th/13th Northumberland Fusiliers (21st Division) faced determined machine gun teams which made any attempt at crossing the Ancre an impossibility during the morning. However, by mid afternoon, 3.30 pm, two companies of the Northumberlands managed to get across and establish themselves at the foot of the slopes beneath Schwaben Redoubt. Further south, from St.Pierre Divion onwards, the story was one of little success for the British troops. The 1st East Yorks were held back until mid evening (8.30 pm) and only one platoon managed to cross the Ancre, in the dead of night, but were soon driven out by counter attack. Facing St.Pierre Divion, north of Hamel, 110 Brigade attacked using the 6th and 7th Leicestershires, but these soldiers could not maintain themselves in the face of accurate trench mortar and machine gun fire from above.

Further south the Welshmen of 113 Brigade (38th Division) were to cross the Ancre at Albert whilst 114 Brigade crossed opposite Hamel. These two Brigades would then converge on Pozieres, leaving the great triangular swathe of ground between the two attacking brigades to be dealt with by 115 Brigade. In the event, within the area attacked by the 38th Division between Hamel and Aveluy, progress proved almost impossible in the waterlogged valley in the face of a strongly held east bank. It was not until the night of 21/22 August that six sections of the 14th Welch got across near to Hamel and occupied a deserted trench in Thiepval Wood, a position which they clung on to until reinforced on the night of 23/24 August.

At the end of 21 August it was clear that any immediate exploitation of any gains achieved by V Corps by cavalry or tanks was impossible.

79

The Ancre valley and the Thiepval positions seen from the Mesnil ridge, west of Aveluy.

The mist had enabled the British infantry to close with those Germans holding the east banks of the Ancre and it was true that very few casualties had been suffered this day. However, sufficient had been done to suggest that the operations of Fourth Army, on either bank of the Somme, should be resumed on 22 August, enabling the 38th and 18th Division to work together in achieving the capture of Albert, the Tara - Usna hills and the Thiepval ridge.

The events of 22 August on the Morlancourt Ridge.

A good location along which it is sensible to view the scene of the events described below is the minor road running south-east from the village of Meaulte, past the British Military Cemetery, towards Etinehem and thence along the D1 in the direction of Bray-sur-Somme. North of Bray the D329 runs back in a north-westerly direction past the southern entrance to Happy Valley and this road also provides good vantage points.

22 August witnessed a major initiative, by III Corps of Fourth Army, astride the Morlancourt ridge. The plan was to advance some two miles across a four mile width of frontage. Four divisions were to be engaged in this attack. On the left, in the low lying ground in the vicinity of Meaulte and Albert the 18th Division were employed ensuring that Bellevue Farm and Vivier Mill were re-captured. On the far right the 3rd Australian Division was to be used adjacent to the River Somme in an attack designed to push past the north of Bray-sur-Somme to their objective at the southern end of Happy Valley (marked as the Vallee du Bois Ricourt on your IGN map). The two divisions in the centre would be the 47th (London) and the 12th (Eastern). It was anticipated that the ridge proper and the ground east of the Bois des Tailles would be captured by the 47th Division operating on the right next to the Australians. To their left would be the 12th Division, adjacent to the 18th Division's men. This advance would take the 47th Division's men

past the grim sight of a large 1916 burial ground, now Grove Town cemetery, which had been established by the 34th and 2/2nd London Casualty Clearing Station on the higher ground of this ridge west of Happy Valley. The advance was to be carried out behind a creeping barrage, made visible to the inexperienced troops by the addition of 7% smoke shells, which would begin at 4.49am and move forward at the rate of 100 yards every four minutes.

Complex arrangements were made to ensure that any success could be exploited by keeping composite brigades with field guns, engineers and machine guns available to move forward at short notice. If the final objectives were captured then III Corps' cavalry, consisting of two squadrons of the 1/1st Northumberland Hussars, as well as a troop of Australian Light Horse and six Whippet tanks, were ordered to take control of the high ground south of Fricourt between Bois Francais and Great Bear Copse. These events would again see extensive use made of tanks. Ten Mark V's of IV Tank Brigade were allotted to the 12th and 47th Divisions whilst the 18th Division was allotted four tanks.

It is a measure of the speed by which the tactics of war had advanced that a great deal of bombing of German targets was undertaken from the air by the Royal Air Force. The night of 21/22nd August was fine and clear, navigation was straightforward. More than twelve tons of bombs were dropped on Cambrai railway station; the sheds at Marcoing station were damaged and the railway bridge at Aubigny-au-Bac was hit. Bombers also struck at the aerodromes at Moislaines and Offoy. The intention was to disrupt the German ability to bring reinforcements forward and to cause chaos in their communications network.

The 47th (2nd London) Division's final objective was Happy Valley, two kilometres north-west of Bray. During 1916 the valley had been an

Mark V tanks during the 1918's fighting south of the Somme in the Australian sector.

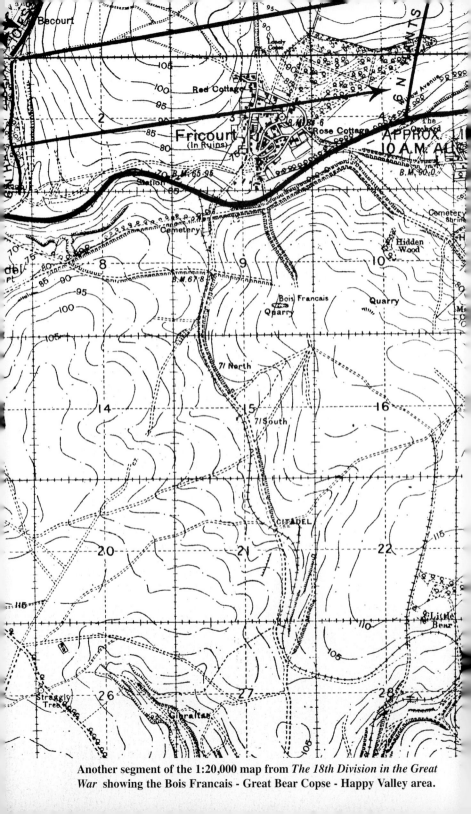

Another segment of the 1:20,000 map from *The 18th Division in the Great War* showing the Bois Francais - Great Bear Copse - Happy Valley area.

important centre for the movement of British troops into and out of the lines during the Battle of the Somme. At its northern end the valley had been terraced around the Gibraltar positions to enable British artillery units to dig into the hillsides in order to fire upon German positions in the Montauban, Guillemont and Ginchy area. At the southern end of the valley, on the D329, is Bray Vale military cemetery which provides a good vantage point from which to consider the attacks undertaken by the 47th Division's men.

Those attacks by the 47th (2nd London) Division fell rather short of achieving their objectives. The Official History noted that 141 Brigade of the 47th Division had a difficult task.

> 'Owing to bad staff work and the insufficient training of the young troops in movements in darkness, smoke, and mist, the two leading battalions, 1/20th and 1/19th London, lost count of distance and though the Germans surrendered freely, the battalions halted considerably short of the intermediate objective, as much as half a mile short on the right.'

142 Brigade following behind had an even more difficult task on its hands and was met by determined resistance. On 142 Brigade's right the 1/22nd Londons got to the southern end of Happy Valley, where Bray Vale cemetery stands today, and made contact with the 33rd Australian battalion. But the other two battalions of 142 Brigade, 1/23rd and 1/24th London, were unable to get forward in the face of German artillery being fired over open sights from the ground above the eastern confines of Happy Valley, that is from positions south of Chataigneraie Farm and along the Fricourt - Bray road towards Bray Hill cemetery. Only one of the tanks allotted to 142 Brigade got as far as Happy Valley, which it entered and then succeeded in rounding up a number of German prisoners before having to be withdrawn because of crew casualties and engine trouble. Happy Valley then became the scene of a disastrous situation which allowed the 1/1st

The view southwards past the two Point 110 Military Cemeteries and the Citadel, from the area of the Bois Francais, towards Chataigneraie Farm.

Northumberland Hussars to ride forward east of Happy Valley without knowledge of what would face them in the vicinity of the Bray - Fricourt road. The Whippet Tanks had already broken down when two squadrons of the Hussars entered Happy Valley from its southern end and headed for the high ground to the north east which in fact was still in German hands. As soon as the leading squadron topped the rise they were met by close range rifle and machine-gun fire as well as bombing from the air! With just 23 men left the squadron rallied under the shelter of the embankments in the Albert - Bray road west of the southern end of Happy Valley where they were joined by the second squadron. Although these unfortunate and inappropriately used mounted soldiers were then withdrawn, the 47th Division's men had no difficulty consolidating their gains across the high ground west of Happy Valley and this day's operations north-west of Bray were therefore concluded by 8.00 am.

North of the 47th Division's men a gap appeared between the 47th and the 12th (Eastern) Division's men on the high ground just to the south of the present day aerodrome south-east of Meaulte. This gap enabled German machine-gunners to enfilade the advance of both divisions, causing many casualties. However, the 12th Division's men were able to take Meaulte, this time somewhat assisted by the effects of the early morning mist which enabled small detachments of soldiers to take many positions by surprise. The investment and capture of Meaulte was achieved by 35 and 36 Brigades with the assistance of a number of tanks. The battalion which actually cleared Meaulte was the 5th Berkshires, assisted by a company of the 6th Northamptonshires (54 Brigade, 18th Division) which co-operated on their left flank.

Thus we can visualise the 12th Division's fight for the Morlancourt

The view looking up Happy Valley which was the scene of the 1/1st Northumberland Hussars' abortive attack on the morning of 22nd August 1918.

Map drawn for the use of the 10 tanks, operating in support of the 12th Division, for the purpose of capturing Meaulte and the Meaulte - Bray road on the morning of 22nd August.

ridge on the right of the 18th Division, with the 38th (Welsh) Division of V Corps of the Third Army on the left of the 18th Division. In this area the Germans were holding the line of the east bank of the Ancre in strength, with Albert as a bridgehead facing and threatening the 18th Division's advance. The general role assigned to the 18th Division was that of covering the flank of the main attack of the Fourth Army by taking the German bridgehead in Albert as well as the high ground east of the town. Within the town's confines the 18th Division's men were instructed to form a defensive flank to protect the northern-most limits of the advance expected to be made by the British 12th and 47th and Australian 3rd Divisions already mentioned.

The Capture of Albert.

The recapture of the town of Albert had enormous significance. It was, undeniably, of great emotional importance given its role in the life of British troops in the second half of 1915 and throughout 1916. More importantly, Albert provided an adequate crossing of the River Ancre and lay along the vital Amiens to Bapaume road which would become instrumental again in moving supplies and munitions to the east during the last 100 days of the war. The story of the recapture of Albert is told in laconic detail in *The 18th Division in the Great War*, G.H.F.Nichols[3], and I have quoted at length from pages 357 - 364 of that book in order to convey and retain the sense of pride and importance which the 18th Division's historian ascribed to those events.[4]

'54 Brigade held the more southerly part of the Divisional line extending from the Ancre about 500 yards east of Dernancourt along the railway to the southern outskirts of Albert; the 6th Northamptons lay on the right, and the 11th Royal Fusiliers on the left, while the 2nd Bedfords were in reserve. 55 Brigade with the 8th East Surreys on the right, the 7th Queens on the left, and 7th Buffs in reserve carried the line northwards through the western out-skirts of the town as far as the Ancre floods between Albert and Aveluy. The western outskirts of Albert had been evacuated by the Germans a fortnight before, but the greater portion of the town was still in his hands and was formidably held. [In 54 Brigade's area overnight patrols managed to position a number of trestle bridges to enable the marshy, shell shattered river course to be crossed. In this area the river course was some two metres deep and four meters in width.]

The attack of the 18th Division was to develop from south to

86

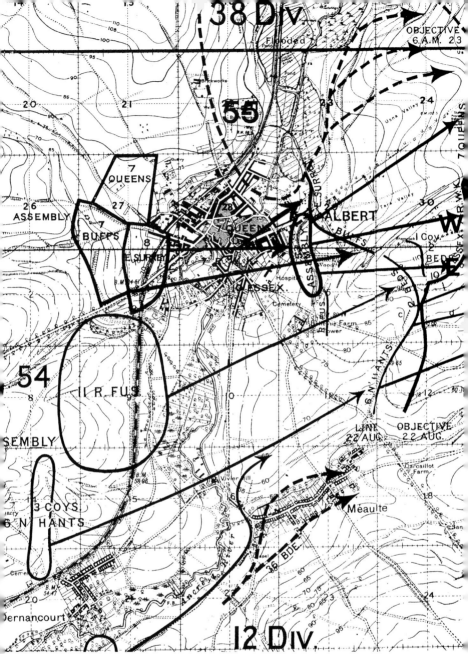

This map is again taken from *The 18th Division in the Great War*, G.H.F.Nichols. This extraordinarily detailed divisional history was published by Blackwood & Sons during 1922. The complete map is from the 1;20,000 series and shows the 18th Division's dispositions in the Albert area during the period 21-22th August 1918.

north. One company of the 6th Northants, aided by four tanks, was to advance at zero hour along the Dernancourt to Meaulte road and gain a footing on the rise east of Vivier Mill, simultaneously with the advance of a battalion of the 12th Division, aided by tanks, to the capture of Meaulte. Whilst this was going on a heavy barrage was to be placed along the Divisional front east of the Ancre until zero plus 30, when that part of it south of Albert would move east to allow the remaining companies of the 6th Northants and the 11th Royal Fusiliers to force a passage of the stream north of Vivier Mill and make the line of the western Albert to Meaulte road while that road was being patrolled by tanks.

The ruins of Albert - as everyone who visited the town during the war will recall - were honeycombed with cellars which offered admirable facilities for defence; and they were cunningly and thoroughly manned and equipped. British patrols had learned the strength of the German resistance on numerous occasions when they had tried to penetrate the town; and it was to be demonstrated once more - happily for the last time - in the obstinate resistance offered on 22nd August.

Further south the crossing of the river was quite likely to prove another hard task, for the Boche had destroyed all the bridges, so that the operation involved the carrying up of bridging material to enable infantry and horse transport to get across a stream some four metres wide and two metres deep, with wet and marshy ground on either bank, heavily cut up by shell-fire, and the enemy waiting in some strength in the neighbourhood of the Albert-Meaulte road.

The objective of the 54th Infantry Brigade was Shamrock Hill and the spur running down to the eastern exit of Meaulte. [Shamrock Hill was the spur of higher ground running into the south east quadrant of Albert from Tara Hill on the Albert - Bapaume road.] To 55th Brigade was allotted the task of capturing the town of Albert, and this operation was divided into three distinct phases.

• First Phase. - Zero to zero plus 60 minutes, when the whole of the town east of the Ancre was submitted to a heavy bombardment. During this period the 8th East Surreys were to work their way to the Ancre, mopping-up such parties of the enemy as were west of the river.

• Second phase. - A heavy bombardment of certain strong

points at the eastern edge of the town, from zero plus 60 minutes to zero plus 120 minutes, during which time the 8th East Surreys were to clear the town east of the Ancre and west of these strong points.

• Third Phase. - At zero plus 120 minutes the bombardment was to lift clear of the town, to allow the 8th East Surreys to complete the capture of the remaining enemy strong points in it.

The next task of 55 Brigade was to gain touch with the left of 54 Brigade, and to form a flank from there to the floods north of Albert; this task was assigned to the 7th Buffs. It was impossible to foresee at what hour this forward movement would become possible, and as it was expected that by that hour Shamrock Hill would be in the hands of 54 Brigade. General Lee decided that the movement should be carried out without cover from a creeping barrage. Four brigades of artillery, the 235th and 236th Brigades of the 47th Divisional Artillery, and the 108th and 175th Army Field Artillery Brigades, and two companies of the 50th Battalion Machine-Gun Corps, in addition to the 18th Division's own Machine Gun battalion under Lieutenant Colonel E.C.T.Minet, were available for the operation.

A brilliant impromptu on the evening of 21st August simplified the next morning's task of 54 Brigade. Patrols succeeded in getting across the river Ancre, and in establishing themselves on the Albert to Meaulte road south of Albert and north of Vivier Mill. A number of light trestle-bridges, constructed by the Divisional Engineers, were then carried to the river and dropped across; and though enemy machine-guns raked the river's course continuously, and in spite of the fact that the night was cloudless with bright moonlight, bodies of the Fusiliers and Northants got over the river. At one point three German machine-guns were firing so persistently that it seemed impossible to bridge the stream, but Private E.G.Hughes, of the Royal Fusiliers, jumped into the water, seized an end of the bridge, and swam and waded until he had placed it in position on the opposite bank. Sergeant C. Robinson of the Northamptonshires performed an almost identical feat. By 2 am so many of our men had crossed that the ground to be swept by our artillery and machine-guns in the opening phase of the barrage programme was already in our possession, and sudden orders had to be issued to meet the altered conditions. It had become certain also that the difficult and possibly very costly operation of forcing the Ancre against severe enemy opposition was now unnecessary.

By zero hour, 4.45 am, sixteen foot-bridges were across the Ancre, and three companies of the 6th Northants, and the whole of the 11th Royal Fusiliers, were formed up on the other side of the Ancre, with the Albert - Meaulte road as their starting line. And here, when the guns burst forth, they waited one hour, the time which had been allowed for the passage of the river. During this time the remaining company of the Northants fought its way forward in the face of heavy opposition, and captured many prisoners and machine-guns on the way.

This having been accomplished, the attack went forward with tanks, under cover of a creeping barrage which played havoc among the German's carefully sited machine-guns, disposed in pairs and in depth along the whole front. Eighty such guns were captured by 54 Brigade, and many more were destroyed by shell-fire. By 8am the Northamptonshires on 54 Brigade's front had practically gained their objective for the day, while the Fusiliers, after overcoming strong opposition from the direction of Albert, Bellevue Farm, and Tara Hill, were holding a line about 500 yards east of Bellevue Farm. Among the captures in the early stage of the proceedings on 54 Brigade's front was a complete German battalion headquarters. In the dug-out was found one of our own men, who had been taken prisoner while on patrol a few hours earlier. He now had the pleasure of escorting the German battalion commander to the cages.

There was no pause. Orders were now received from General Lee that on the final objective being reached, strong fighting patrols should be pushed forward, and the ground thus reconnoitred made good by companies following in close support. This was duly acted upon by the Bedfordshires and Northamptonshires; and in the meantime the 8th Royal Berkshires (temporarily placed under the command of Brigadier General Sadleir-Jackson, G.O.C. 54 Brigade) were also moved across the Ancre to support the further advance. Meanwhile the Fusiliers, who had been plugging away in the centre, found this left flank held up by German machine - guns, principally from a strong point on the summit of Shamrock Hill, an elevation directly east of Albert, and overlooking the level land south of the town. As a result they had to dig in. During the afternoon, however, a company of the 2nd Bedfords, ably led by Captain

R.L.V.Doake, passed through the Fusiliers, captured the hill point, silenced its gunners, and enabled the Fusiliers to proceed.

In the meantime, on 55 Brigade's front, the capture of Albert had been proceeding according to plan, and by 9.10am the 8th East Surreys - to whom the task of storming and clearing the town had been entrusted had finished their job, after nearly four and a half hours determined fighting, much of it in the town itself.

[The town of Albert was thus regained finally.] *Albert was ours again; but it was a tragically unfamiliar Albert in which the men found themselves in the glare of that day's hot August sun. Streets, once picturesque and lively with the business of British military life, had become mere paths littered with rubbish, lined with stumps of walls and wrecks of buildings, and undermined in every direction with land-mines and charges. The basilica, from which the golden image of the Virgin and Child had hung for so long[5], was there yet, and its vast nave still dominated the town, but it had become a mere huge forbidding shell of red brick. In front of it lay a wrecked German plane, and here and farther on, near the Singer factory, dead British patrols; and everywhere were German dead. One felt that the only fit setting for such a scene was absolute stillness - the silence of the grave. But beyond the town the noise of battle still went on. And inside the ruins one could hear and see Colonel Symons's sappers at work*

The Basilica in Albert after its re-capture.

rendering harmless the land-mines left by the enemy under every road and bridge; 136 land-mines and charges they removed that day, and they did the work so thoroughly that not a single accident occurred. The Boche had done his best and bravest; but it was difficult not to feel, as one looked around the hideous wreckage of what once had been a pleasant, stately little town,

A street in Albert photographed just after the Germanshad been pushed out by the 18th Division's men.

that he had found a fitting tomb.

The battle progressed rapidly. The attack had attained its object. The Bedfords were on Shamrock Hill by 10 am; the East Surreys had 'mopped-up' Albert; the 6th Northants, on the right, were in touch with 86 Brigade of the 12th Division; and, on the left, the 7th Buffs, debouching from Albert, joined near Black Wood with the 2nd Bedfords, who were in support of the 11th Royal Fusiliers. The Buffs, who after the 8th August fighting had received two large drafts - chiefly coal miners and munition workers, all men of fine fighting quality - were also better provided with company commanders than they had been for a long time. Captains Stronge, Nicholas, and Whitmarsh were all experienced officers who commanded their companies at all times, whether in or out of the line; and, with so many new young officers and men in the battalion, their qualities of leadership counted for much. When the Buffs debouched from Albert without a barrage, and advanced over open ground, enemy machine-guns on Tara Hill met them with a merciless fire, and the leading companies lost heavily - especially 'C' Company, whose

company commander, Lieutenant Barber, a very excellent officer, was wounded. Captain Whitmarsh was most conspicuous in this advance. He rallied his men, and by skilful tactics methodically moved forward to Black Wood, and, in spite of heavy shelling and machine-gun fire, held that valuable point until dark. But his company lost all its other officers, and suffered over 60 per cent in casualties.

The end of a long and significant day's fighting found the line stretching from the railway, just north of Meaulte as far as the Ancre floods between Albert and Aveluy, with a generous and safe curve in the right direction - the east. Many hundreds of prisoners had fallen to our share: the Northamptonshires had taken 670, and the East Surreys 110 in Albert. General Lee and all concerned could look back upon a satisfactory Divisional contribution to the opening stages of the great battle of Bapaume, which was to keep the Allies victoriously busy for the next nine days.'

The 18th Division's casualties incurred during the recapture of Albert are buried within the Albert Communal Cemetery Extension, close to the roadside in a small elevated section on your left as you pass through the entrance. Another group of the 18th Division's men are buried on the reverse slope of Shamrock Hill within Becourt Military Cemetery.

During the afternoon of 22nd August there were various attempts by the Germans to disrupt the advanced forces of the 47th Division on the Morlancourt Ridge. To some extent these succeeded in pushing some units of 142 Brigade back until they rejoined the soldiers of 141 Brigade in what had been the intermediate objectives of the day's advance. Nevertheless, the Fourth Army had obliterated the German salient on the ridge east of Morlancourt and had re-captured Albert and the important railheads to the south.

During the night of 22/23rd August soldiers of the 15th (Carmarthen Battalion) Welsh Regiment managed to get across the Ancre north of Thiepval Wood and established a position near to St.Pierre Divion which they clung onto despite repeated German counter attacks. On the morning of 23rd August various operations drove the German Army

94

further from Albert. These were undertaken by the 18th Division working in conjunction with the 38th (Welsh) Division. The 38th Division were deployed in the angle between the Albert to Bapaume road and the River Ancre and attacked at 4.45 am towards the Usna Hill, crossing that and securing their objectives. From here the 38th Division's men could look across Mash Valley towards the devastated villages of Ovillers and La Boisselle. Meanwhile the 18th Division was only able to progress some 1000 yards east of Albert and were left below the summit of Tara Hill. Some progress was also made on the banks of the Somme towards the south of Bray-sur-Somme by soldiers of the 3rd Australian Division. This day the 47th and 12th Division's men were not engaged in the fighting.

During the night of 23/24th the two remaining companies of the 15th Welsh as well as the entirety of the 14th Welsh (Swansea) Battalion got across the Ancre in the Thiepval Wood and St.Pierre Divion areas. Most of the 14th battalion's men had to wade across up to their necks in the water as they prepared to attack the heights of

Meaulte village. 23rd August 1918. The Official Photographer at work.

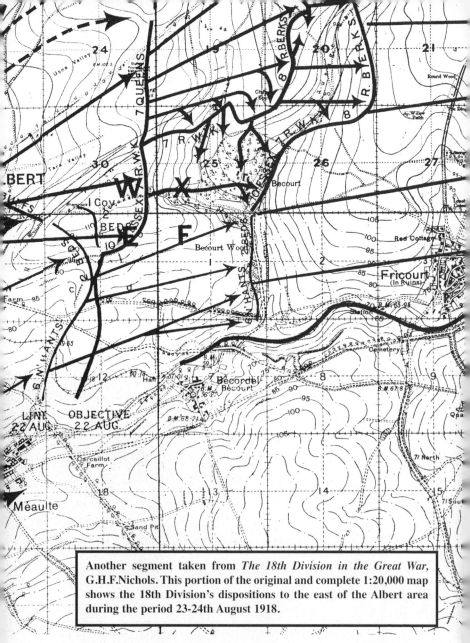

Another segment taken from *The 18th Division in the Great War*, G.H.F.Nichols. This portion of the original and complete 1:20,000 map shows the 18th Division's dispositions to the east of the Albert area during the period 23-24th August 1918.

Thiepval. At the same time 115 Brigade crossed the Ancre via a bridge constructed at Aveluy. At 1.00 am the assault of the 38th Division was launched resulting in the recapture of the high ground north of Thiepval (Schwaben Redoubt) and Thiepval village by 114 Brigade. Subsequently 113 and 115 Brigades pressed past La Boisselle and

Ovillers and ended this day having captured 634 prisoners and 143 machine guns. It was measure of how the balance of morale had swung in the Welshmen's favour that the German Army should prove capable of losing so many machine guns on just one day to a division advancing across such disadvantageous terrain.

It is worth mentioning the Y Sap crater here at La Boisselle which was once again the scene of intense fighting. It was not until 8.00 pm on 24th August that the 8th Royal Berks (53 Brigade, 18th Div.) drove the Germans eastwards from its' confines.

Early that same morning, 24th August, Bray-sur-Somme had been secured by the 3rd Australian Division's men. Alongside the 38th Division's attacks the Australians' attacks had been launched at 1.00 am, in bright moonlight. However, as the morning unfolded the weather became cloudy and cooler, drizzle setting in until, by midday, low cloud and poor visibility made all arms co-operation with the RAF difficult. Nevertheless, Becourt village and Becourt Wood also fell to the soldiers of the 18th Division. During this day the 12th and 47th

Aerial Photograph. The La Boisselle - Lochnagar area in the summer of 1918.

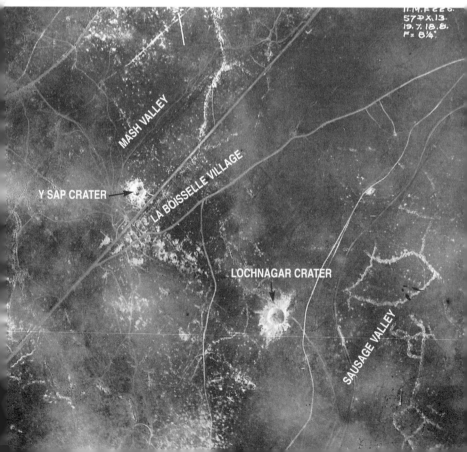

Divisions were also re-engaged. The area around Happy Valley and the higher ground on the ridge south-east of Meaulte then saw heavy fighting involving both the 12th and 47th as well as the 58th Division, some of whose troops were used from reserve[6]. Although more than 300 German prisoners were captured within Happy Valley by soldiers of the 1/15th London (47th Division) the high ground near to Grove Town cemetery was the scene of intense fighting after a gap again appeared between the 12th and 47th Divisions at this location during the early morning's advance. The cause of this problem was two strong points being manned by soldiers of the German 115th Regiment of the 25th Division. Their machine guns caused havoc amongst the men of the 6th Royal West Kents and 6th Queen's as well as the 21st Londons. Three tanks from the 1st Tank Battalion were deployed in order to clear up the situation but their attempts failed, two being disabled and the third tank's guns jamming. It was not until 6.00 pm that the ground north-west of Grove Town cemetery was captured, by which time the positions of Becordel - Becourt and Happy Valley were secure.

The subsequent advance of the 18th (Eastern) Division.

During 25th August the remains of Becourt Wood, Fricourt and Mametz villages were re-captured by the 18th Division's men. There is a very poignant small group of graves, belonging to 83 men killed

Bray-sur-Somme, viewed down the valley cut into the plateau south of Fricourt near to the site of The Loop.

whilst serving with the 18th Division at the start of this period, within Becourt Military Cemetery. That cemetery lies due east of Albert on the reverse slope of Shamrock Hill which the 18th had attacked immediately after capturing Albert. South of Fricourt the Bois Francais and The Citadel were captured by the 12th Division. The 18th were the northernmost unit operating under the command of Fourth Army. To their north were the 38th Division, V Corps, Third Army. The speed of this extraordinary success clearly marks the establishment of fluid and open mobile warfare. Thus, soon after its success at Albert the 18th Division found itself fighting across its old July 1916 battlefield, this time past Danzig Alley, Mametz Wood and Pommiers Redoubt towards Montauban, although now from west to east rather than south to north as in July 1916. Montauban was captured by the 7th Buffs on the evening of the 26th, under the command of Captain A.J.Whitmarsh whose handling of the young troops brought him the D.S.O for his

The Bernafay - Trones Woods attack. 18th Div Hist.

efforts this day. In his enterprise Whitmarsh's men were also aided by the 11th Royal Fusiliers who moved into Montauban from the south-west.

After the capture of Montauban it is worth noting that the 8th Berkshires received a draft of eight officers who went immediately into action - the most severe opposition being met by the 18th Division in the vicinity of Bernafay and Trones Woods the following day. During the summer of 1916 these locations had acquired notoriety during the fighting for the approaches to Guillemont. Now, on Tuesday 27th August 1918, it was the scene of a parallel assault which mirrored both the direction and difficulties which the 30th Division's men had experienced during the first fortnight of July 1916. Once again it was the village of Longueval, to the north of Trones Wood, which held the answer. The 18th Division's plans were for an advance across the north of Bernafay and Trones Woods before wheeling inwards to capture the woods. This manoeuvre was thought practicable because the Longueval - Bazentin ridge was believed to be in the hands of the 38th (Welsh) Division. (See also the events surrounding 122 Brigade Royal Field Artillery at Longueval.) The attack began at 4.55 am. Within minutes it was clear that the bulk of the casualties incurred during this action were going to be suffered by the 8th Royal Berkshires, operating on the left flank, because the Germans were now re-established within Longueval.

Whilst the 7th Royal West Kents advanced on the right with few casualties the Berkshires were devastated by machine gun fire from the ridge between Caterpillar Valley Cemetery[7] and the southern part of Longueval. Incidentally, Caterpillar Valley Cemetery is a fine vantage point. It was later begun by units of the 38th Welsh division whose casualties from the Longueval fighting are buried towards the left of the cemetery, the rest of which is formed from battlefield clearances and concentrations after the war - the bulk of those buried having been killed during 1916. The cemetery is also the site of an important New Zealand Division memorial to their 1,205 missing, during the fighting of September and October 1918, north and east of here.

Throughout the morning of 27th the situation ebbed and flowed as German counter attacks sought to clear the weak parties of Berkshires

Trones and Bernafay Woods pictured from the road to Montauban from Hardecourt-aux-Bois.

The 18th (Eastern) Division's memorial at Trones Wood, north of Maltz Horn Farm.

from the north of Trones Wood and then, by a battalion of Prussian Guards, the southern end of the wood - an attack which succeeded in driving the 18th Division's men back into the eastern perimeter of Bernafay Wood. A further attack by the Essex and Berks was mounted later at 7.00 pm and this, against the odds, succeeded in driving the

The 18th Division's advance past the village of Guillemont. 18th Div Hist.

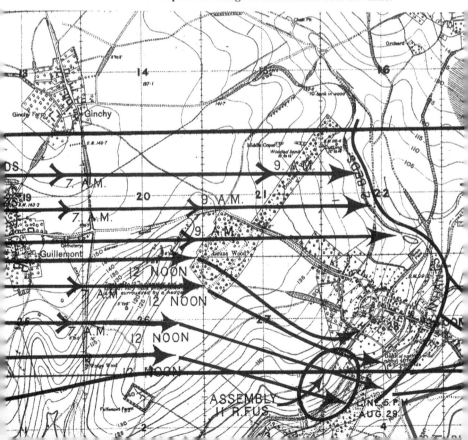

The 18th Division's attack on Rancourt and St Pierre Vaast Wood. 18th Div Hist.

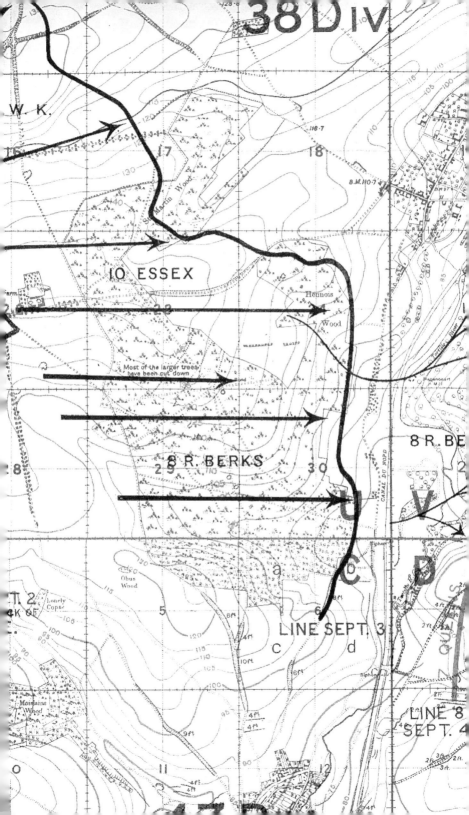

Looking past the archetypal Somme village of Hardecourt-aux-Bois, from the Maricourt-Hardecourt road, north-eastwards in the direction of Leuze Wood and Combles.

Germans from Trones Wood. Of the eight newly arrived officers who had been rushed into action with the Berkshires, 'two were killed, three were wounded, one was hit going back to "Battle Surplus", one fell sick going up the line, one fought and came through.'

By 29th August the 18th Division were in Combles having passed what their divisional history called 'the dreary waste of battered Nissen huts, gaping holes, and heaps of broken bricks still entered on the maps as the village of Guillemont.'! Having left Trones Wood at 5.15 am and passed Guillemont soon afterwards the 18th Division's men were in the western edge of Leuze Wood at 9.00 am. Thereafter this day was marked by escalating artillery exchanges and the day ended with the 18th's men north and south of Combles - but not within. Whilst Combles had fallen without a struggle in 1916, this time the German defence was resilient.

On 30th little progress was made since German F.O.O.s, looking down from the Morval Ridge, ensured that British troop movements were quickly engaged by German artillery pieces under their control. 1st September saw a set piece advance which was designed to secure the Morval, Combles and Sailly Saillisel area. In this enterprise the 38th were to capture Morval and Sailly Saillisel, whilst the 18th moved forward through Combles to a position astride the Rancourt to Sailly Saillisel road down to the north-western portion of St Pierre Vaast Wood. On the 18th's right the 47th Division were to take Rancourt and the south-east corner of St Pierre Vaast Wood.

The following day, 1st September, the 18th's men secured the north eastern portions of St Pierre Vaast Wood. By the 2nd Governement Farm was occupied and Vaux Wood on 3rd. On 4th September patrols of men from the 18th crossed the Canal du Nord, the Tortille River and occupied Riverside Wood to the south of Manancourt. That day the 18th were taken out of the line and replaced by the 12th who immediately took up the pursuit, harrying the Germans back onto the Nurlu plateau. During those two weeks between 22nd August and 5th September the 18th Division had fought continuously. They had achieved something which their 1916 forebears would have regarded as the impossible. In doing that their casualties had been remarkably light:

	Killed.	Wounded.	Missing.	Total.
Officers:	21	102	2	125
Other Ranks:	330	1947	450	2727

The advance of the 12th (Eastern) Division.

Moving parallel to and south of the 18th Division the route taken by the 12th Division during the month of August took them from positions west of Morlancourt and south of Dernancourt to positions south of Combles by 29th August. That constituted approximately an 18 kilometre (12 mile) advance across terrain made technically difficult by the latticework of entrenchments and wire obstacles which snaked across almost every part of the ground here. During the first three days of that advance progress was measured and had foundered in front of Hill 105 south of Meaulte. Today's IGN maps identify the prominence as being 108 metres above sea level! The events of 22nd August, during the first day of the Battle of Albert proper, saw the 12th Division pass Hill 105 and move forward astride the D329 Meaulte - Bray road near to the Sand Pit. The Sand Pit can be found easily half way between the aerodrome on the D329 and the Aerospatiale works east of Meaulte. It was here, in the midst of the first day of open warfare, that Sergeant Trevor, of the 9th Royal Fusiliers, entered one

Taken from the 12th Division's history (pp198), showing the incredible advance across Meaulte, Becordel and the Morlancourt Ridge, past the Citadel, Carnoy, Hardecourt and Maurepas during August 1918.

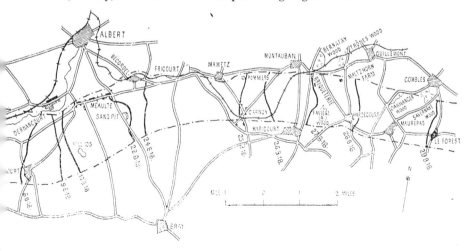

The Bois Francais area on the north of the 12th Division's advance on the 25th August.

German dugout alone only to emerge moments later with thirty more prisoners.

On 25th August the night and early morning was exceptionally foggy and visibility was less than 50 metres. With the German Army in full retreat the 12th Division's advance was renewed at 2.30 am with officers giving directions using maps and compass. The whole division moved forwards against very limited opposition, covering two miles before 7.15 am! Not one casualty was incurred throughout the entire manoeuvre. The advance of the 12th Division was covered by the cavalry of XXIInd Corps who were operating on the high ground between Carnoy and Montauban. During the following 56 hours the fighting in the area of Maltz Horn Farm, Hardecourt and Faviere Wood was severe. One battalion whose part here is noteworthy was the 9th Royal Fusiliers. The battalion had just received a large draft to replace losses incurred during the opening days of the Battles of Amiens and Albert. Those 350 recruits, still in their first week in France, were composed entirely of men aged between eighteen and nineteen and a half years of age. On 28th August the battalion was faced by experienced units of the German Fusilier Guards yet still managed to behave with great gallantry, clearing Faviere Wood, occupying Hardecourt, capturing droves of prisoners and sixteen machine guns. It was an incredible, vivid and difficult experience for youngsters whose descendants today would still be at secondary school.

One casualty which saddened his unit greatly was Lieutenant Colonel Saint, D.S.O., of the 1/1st Cambridgeshires. During the afternoon of 28th August Saint was mortally wounded by shellfire and died the following day. Edward Twelftree Saint had arrived, with the battalion, in France during February 1915 as a company commander and had been given command of his battalion in September 1917.

106

The subsequent advance in this sector after 30th August was carried forward by the 47th Division, which had been brought back into the line to relieve the 12th Division who themselves took over the advance from the 18th Division after the Canal du Nord had been crossed on 4th September.

The 38th (Welsh) Division's advance across the 1916 battlefield to the Canal du Nord.

This division was operating under the command of V Corps, Third Army. On their southern flank were the 18th Division - the northern unit of Fourth Army, whilst on their north were the 17th (Northern) Division. The advance of the 38th Division during the period 24th August to early September reads like a roll call of the many locations noted for the severity of fighting which occurred there in the summer of 1916. We have already seen how the division had captured the Thiepval heights as well as La Boisselle and Ovillers on 24th August. Later that day the division's men advanced on and secured Contalmaison and reached Pozieres.

The following day, 25 August, the division moved forward across the highest ground on the Somme battlefield with three brigades in line abreast, closely followed by the entirety of their artillery, to find German lines of resistance between Mametz Wood and High Wood. Mametz Wood was taken by 113 Brigade. The 2nd Royal Welsh Fusiliers and the 10th South Wales Borderers captured Bazentin-le-Petit whilst the 14th and 15th Welsh took the high ground south of the village of Martinpuich. Unfortunately it proved impossible to threaten High Wood (Bois des Fourcaux on your IGN map) until subsequent advances by 113 and 115 Brigades.

During the early hours of 26th August 113 Brigade fought their way across towards the western limits of Longueval's shattered outlines, where they subsequently held on throughout the day in the face of counter attacks which were massed unseen within the confines of Delville Wood. Unfortunately 113 Brigade were unable to clear the Longueval ridge, just west of the village, of all its hidden machine guns. Simultaneously 115 Brigade advanced across the north side of Longueval. By the following morning, 27th August, 115 were 'leapfrogged' by 114 which was able to move forward at 4.00 am to reach the D197 Flers road on the north of High Wood. Later that afternoon the Longueval - High Wood area witnessed an extraordinary and gallant action by 122 Brigade Royal Field Artillery. According to the Divisional History

'About 2 p.m. 122nd Brigade, Royal Field Artillery, was ordered to advance into action in the valley west of High Wood, in support of our Infantry who were advancing. Later it transpired that the enemy held the Longueval ridge in force. It was decided, however, to get the guns forward. There was only one possible route - the Bazentin - High Wood road which was narrow, made of planks, and in full view for 500 yards where it passed over the plateau between Bazentin and Martinpuich. One battery got through untouched but then two 5.9" batteries were turned on to the road and put down a barrage 300 yards in depth, through which the remaining three batteries had to pass. This was accomplished by galloping down the road by sections at a time. There were direct hits on seven different teams, but the whole brigade got into action a few hundred yards west of High Wood. The limbers and teams passed back to the rear through the barrage which, though now not so heavy, caused further casualties. Shortly afterwards information was received that a strong hostile counter-attack was developing from the northern edge of Delville Wood. This was engaged by the brigade at 1000-1500 yards' range and definitely broken up. During this action the guns were under machine-gun fire from the right flank and

Here British soldiers pursue the exhausted German forces following the Battle of Albert.

also were engaged by a 77mm. battery which was in action just east of Longueval cross roads and firing over open sights and about 1500 yards' range causing many casualties.

Several further counter-attacks were made against the Infantry that evening but all were driven off by the combined fire of our Artillery and Infantry and of 'B' and 'D' Machine-Gun Companies.'

This action is a very simple one to visualise and is the subject of an attractive and easy walk. The nearby visitor's centre at Delville Wood are able to provide refreshments and seats if need be afterwards! Throughout 28th August heavy artillery fire was poured into the Delville Wood area in order to soften the German's resistance. However the Welshmen were able to get little respite since the German artillery responded in kind. At the end of a long and stressful day of artillery duelling the Germans were seen to be weakening. Seizing the initiative 113 Brigade were ordered forward and drove the German army from Longueval for the last time. *(Map - Walk 4)*

The following morning, 29th August, 113 Brigade moved forward from positions adjacent to the military cemetery south of Delville Wood in order to prepare for the capture of Ginchy village. On the other side of the devastated wood 115 Brigade moved past the north of Delville leaving the process of clearing the wood to the 13th Battalion Welsh Regiment. The 38th Division then attacked and captured the

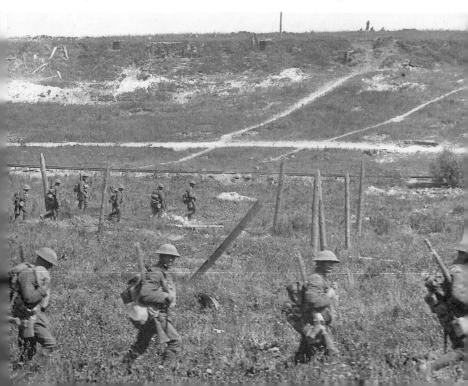

Ginchy positions to the east of Delville Wood. That evening the 38th Division's men captured Lesboeufs, to the north-east of Ginchy, but were held up by strong forces in the village of Morval to the south of Lesboeufs. The following day, 30th, was one of intense artillery exchanges and heavy casualties amongst the infantry as all attempts to capture Morval failed. At this point the division paused for breath whilst the artillery reduced the Morval positions to rubble. At 4.45 am on 1st September Morval was attacked and captured by 114 Brigade amidst enormously intense fighting. The village of Morval is the site of a unique cemetery, constructed here by a burial party of the 38th Division. Although constructed within the confines of the 1916 battlefield there is not one 1916 casualty buried within! Later the same day the village of Sailly Saillisel (located on the N17 east of the A1-E15 motorway) was captured - the men advancing so rapidly that their supply and support required superhuman efforts to keep pace.

By this stage the move across the old 1916 battlefield had been almost completed. The 38th Division was approaching the obstacle of the Canal du Nord at the village of Etricourt - Manancourt. The crossing of the Canal du Nord here, on 4th September, was a magnificent feat of arms, a story which deserves to be re-told.

'The canal here is an impassable obstacle, and it looked as if the advance might have been checked for some time had it not been for one of the most brilliant Infantry actions of the Advance, which was performed by the 13th Welsh Regiment the next day, under the personal direction of Major Hobbs.

The enemy had machine guns on the bank but not covering the actual water; noticing this, Major Hobbs rushed a platoon down to an old trench on the near bank, from which a ditch led down towards the debris of the Etricourt road bridge. Here the platoon engaged the attention of the nearest machine guns and one section crawled down the ditch across the fallen bridge and up the far bank; crawling on their stomachs this section advanced to within charging distance of the nearest machine gun, then leapt up and bayoneted the gunners. They were quickly joined by the remainder of the platoon and a bridgehead was formed which enabled the remainder of the company (under Capt. Beech, M.C.) to cross.

Similar action took place at Manancourt where a company of the 14th Welsh Regiment, led by Major J.A.Daniels, D.S.O., M.C., of the 15th Welsh (attached to the 14th) crossed, and each of these battalions had thus one company across by 11.30 a.m.;

these companies cleared the eastern bank of the enemy and then pushed forward to cover the crossing of the remainder of the Brigade, which was effected with the help of the 123rd Field Company, R.E., by 5 p.m. This Field Company worked continuously throughout the afternoon and night and the following day; they were under shell fire the whole time, and had to perform the whole of the work in gas masks; and sustained thirty casualties; it was owing to their efforts that our relief by the 21st Division the following night and their subsequent advance was made possible.

During the day the remainder of the Divisional Artillery advanced in close support and came into action on the forward slopes south of Mesnil; in order to do this they also had to move

Taken from the 18th Divisional History showing the Etricourt - Manancourt positions.

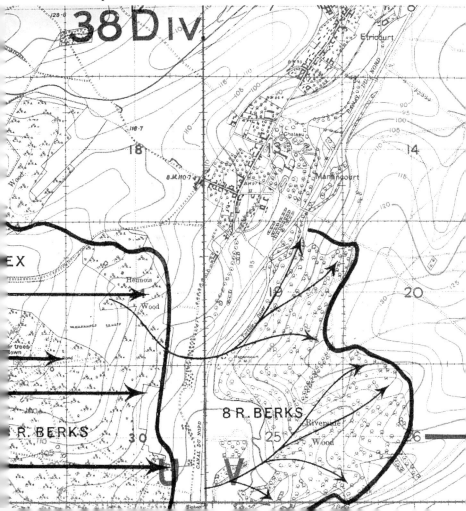

across the open from Sailly Saillisel in full view from the enemy's
position about Equancourt; that such a movement was possible
without prohibitive casualties is probably due to the action of the
17th Division on our left, which was engaging part of the
enemy's attention at the time. A section of 'D' Machine Gun
Company crossed this ground at the gallop this day in order to
reinforce the remainder of the machine guns which had either
moved forward by night or had been carried forward by hand.

All guns and vehicles approaching our forward troops had to
move through Sailly Saillisel as, being the only road, the site of
this village was under continual shell fire and it speaks well for
the march discipline of artillery and transport that nothing in the
nature of a block ever occurred in the traffic.' [10]

Thereafter the 38th (Welsh) Division were relieved by the 21st
Division. The artillery remained in action but the infantry and their
support units now had six days' badly needed rest, for they had been
continuously engaged for more than a fortnight, during which time
they had driven the enemy back for a distance of 15 miles; capturing
twenty-nine officers, 1,886 other ranks, six guns and many machine
guns. The 38th had suffered 3,014 casualties during the two weeks.
During this period the Divisional Artillery (with the 62nd Artillery
attached) had been continuously on the move in close support of the
infantry and had fired over three hundred thousand rounds - one third
of a million shells! The logistics of this move were extraordinary and
involved hugely lengthy supply lines. The 38th Division's railhead was
maintained at Ferme Rosel, on the Amiens - Doullens road, and only
moved forward briefly to Aveluy when the forward troops were east of
the Canal du Nord! During that period the horse drawn and motorised
convoys supplying the 38th's men had shuttled backwards and
forwards across a battlefield wasteland devastated by four and a half
years of conflict.

A Victoria Cross for Sergeant Colley of the Lancashire Fusiliers.

I have included details of this action as representative of the part
played by the 17th (Northern) Division's men who were operating
north of the 38th Division. I have drawn on details contained within the
Lancashire Fusiliers' marvellous regimental history[11].

Harold Colley's Victoria Cross was the Regiment's fifteenth in the
war. The 10th Battalion, commanded by Lieutenant Colonel
R.E.Cotton, had been in and near to Aveluy Wood for some weeks and
was in reserve near Acheux on 23rd August when it received orders to

move forward to its old trenches facing the River Ancre. During that night the Germans began to retire and the battalion moved forward early on the 24th, crossing the Ancre by a much-damaged causeway over the marshy ground on both sides of the stream, which had to be waded. The advance was continued, behind the 10th West Yorkshire Regiment, to the high ground north of Thiepval. In 1916 that high ground was the Schwaben Redoubt, today the site of La Grande Ferme on your IGN map. In the afternoon the battalion was ordered to continue its advance towards Courcelette. Owing to some loss of direction by other units, the leading companies of the 10th found themselves eventually alongside, instead of behind, the West Yorkshire, and encountered strong opposition from the direction of that village. After an order to advance towards Martinpuich had been cancelled, the battalion took up a position for the night on a line running north and south about a mile south-west of Courcelette. Thus on the night of 23/24th August the 10th LFs were between Courcelette and Pozieres facing east.

At 1.30 a.m., on 24th, orders were received for an eastward thrust to take place at 4 a.m., with Martinpuich as the first objective, the 12th Manchester Regiment passing to the south and the 10th Lancashire Fusiliers to the north of the village, joining hands on the far side and then 'mopping up' within Martinpuich itself. The village was strongly held with machine guns and the Germans shelled the advancing troops heavily, causing a number of casualties. The garrison was eventually driven out, but the shelling prevented any British troops remaining in the village. Later B (Captain T.Howarth, M.C.) and D (Captain F.W.Brittnell) companies of the 10th LFs secured a foothold in the trenches north of the village. Second-Lieutenant L.G.Holgate led his platoon with great gallantry and was largely instrumental in securing the success of the attack. He was seriously wounded but refused to be moved to the rear until three even more seriously wounded men had been carried to the aid post. The advance continued in the afternoon, with C (Captain L.H.Gibbs) and A (Captain I.Sankey) leading and B and D in support. The two leading companies diverged somewhat during their advance, and B and D again found themselves in the leading line. When the troops reached a crest about half a mile to the east of Martinpuich, a large body of Germans, estimated at three companies, was seen advancing down the forward slope of the next ridge deployed for a counter-attack. The 10th Battalion quickly manned some handy trenches, even the battalion headquarters extending the line under the personal leadership of Lieutenant-Colonel

Cotton, before the Germans were on them at about 4.15 p.m. At this moment, four machine guns of the 17th Machine Gun Company happened to arrive, and with their aid the counter-attack was eventually stopped, though it was pressed with great determination and with the evident intention of retaking Martinpuich.

The garrison of an advanced trench hastily occupied by B Company suffered particularly heavy casualties. Sergeant Harold Colley, M.M., of that company, grasping the situation, rushed forward on his own initiative to help them, and rallied and controlled them. By this time the enemy had already obtained a lodgement in the trench. Colley formed a defensive flank, held up the enemy, and eventually drove them out. Only three men of the garrison were by this time unwounded, and Colley himself was so dangerously wounded that he died that night. It was entirely due to his action that the enemy were prevented from breaking through and his courage and tenacity saved a very critical situation and won for him a posthumous Victoria Cross. Another gallant act at this time was performed by Corporal G. Thomas, who went out with an officer to within fifty yards of the enemy and killed three of them as they were bringing a machine gun into action. He then brought back information which enabled fire to be directed at the vital points of the enemy's line and thus contributed most usefully to the stopping of the attack. This resulted in Thomas' winning the DCM.

But the battalion was not disposed to rest content with merely stopping the enemy's progress. At about 7 p.m. Captain T.Howarth, M.C., led some thirty men of 'B' Company in an attempt to dislodge two machine guns on the left of the battalion's front. But although his leadership was skilful and he showed a fine disregard of danger, the fire of German machine guns elsewhere was too strong for him and the attempt had to be abandoned. At dusk Private J. Cadman, of battalion headquarters, went out and, observing two of the enemy isolated, brought them back as prisoners. During the night the battalion re-formed behind the 9th Duke of Wellington's Regiment, which had passed through the line at 1 a.m. to continue the attack in the direction of Flers. As the 26th August progressed, the German resistance stiffened once more, and in the afternoon the 10th LFs was ordered to try to pass through the 12th Manchesters which had attempted an outflanking movement, but the only result was serious congestion in the forward positions and no progress. After dark the battalion relieved the Manchesters in the line, and was later relieved itself.

The casualties amongst the 10th Lancashire Fusiliers during this period were 1 officer and 50 men killed, 4 officers and 150 men wounded, 1 officer wounded and missing and 18 men missing.

Sergeant Harold John Colley is buried within Mailly Wood Cemetery. Colley, who came from Birmingham, was clearly an exceptionally brave soldier having already won the Military Medal. For those of you interested in locating the scenes of Victoria Cross actions you might like to know that another soldier serving with the Lancashire Fusiliers had won both the DCM and the fourteenth of the Lancashire Fusiliers' Victoria Crosses within two weeks of each award just a few miles north of here. That soldier was Lance Sergeant Edward Smith who was serving with the 1/5th LFs (42nd Division). His DCM was awarded as a result of patrol actions on 10th August in the area of Touvent Farm between Hebuterne and Serre and his VC as a result of actions on 21st August at Beauregard. He was nineteen years of age and survived the war. It is remarkable to think that two VCs should be awarded to members of the same regiment in such proximity, and also that Smith should win both the DCM and VC within 11 days of each other.

Lance Sergeant Edward Smith who served with the 1/5th LFs, photographed in 1918 and later during the 1930s.

• • • •

Thus, within days of the Battle of Albert commencing the Fourth Army's soldiers were overlooking Peronne on the River Somme, by 29th August, whilst the Third Army's soldiers had captured Bapaume, on 30th August. Incredibly, given where they had commenced two weeks earlier, the 38th Division's men were across the Canal du Nord, north-east of Peronne, by 4th September with the 18th Division's men on their right towards Moislaines. Within those two weeks a huge tract of territory had been crossed and made secure, including the entirety of the 1916 Somme battlefield, by a British Army making use of all arms tactics capable of being followed by a nucleus of battle-hardened troops and the many youthful and inexperienced conscripts who now appeared in great numbers within every infantry unit.

During these two weeks the German Army were given no respite, little sleep and few opportunities to place any distance between themselves and the attentions of both the Third and Fourth Armies. From their commencement east of Amiens, across the Morlancourt Ridge, through Albert and past the villages of Meaulte, Pozieres and soon after Maurepas and Rancourt these events at the start of the last 'One Hundred Days' of the Great War witnessed the rapid evolution of mobile warfare. Even as September days began to shorten it was clear that war had finally left these villages and the processes of civilian re-occupation would begin soon. Initially the villages became the grim scene of battlefield clearance teams' work, but by the summer of 1919 the French population began to make their way wearily home, commencing the process of transforming a devastated wasteland into that fertile source of sugar beet and root crops which it had always been in the decades prior to 1914.

1. V Corps consisted of three divisions, the 17th, 21st and the 38th.

2. *London Gunners*. Kingham. Methuen & Co Ltd. 1919.

3. *The 18th Division in the Great War*, G.H.F.Nichols, William Blackwood & Sons, Edinburgh and London, 1922.

4. On a small number of occasions I have tidied the grammar, split lengthy paragraphs, deleted a small number of words and metricated dimensions in order to make the passage more readable.

5. The statue of the Golden Virgin and Child had previously been removed from the summit of the basilica's tower by the artillery of the 35th Division on 16 April 1918. The Divisional History (Lieutenant Colonel H.M.Davson, pub. Sifton Praed & Co, London, 1926) says of that event; '....the prophesy that its fall would herald the end of the war was not fulfilled with any suddenness.'

6. The 58th Division fades from this narrative because two of its Brigades, 174 and 175, were placed under the command of the 18th and 47th Divisions during the first few days of their advance eastwards.

7. So named by the 38th Division's burial party because the site overlooked Caterpillar Valley. It would more effectively be named Longueval Ridge cemetery.

8. *The 18th Division in the Great War*, G.H.F.Nichols, William Blackwood & Sons, Edinburgh and London, 1922,

9. *A History of the 38th (Welsh) Division*. Ed: Mumby. Hugh Rees Ltd. London. 1922.

10. *A History of the 38th (Welsh) Division*. Ed: Mumby. Hugh Rees Ltd. London. 1922.

11. *The History of the Lancashire Fusiliers. 1914 - 1918*. Latter. Gale & Polden. Aldershot. 1949.

Chapter Five

THE CEMETERIES AND MEMORIALS

The cemeteries and memorials within the area covered by this guide are multitudinous, their numbers a shock to all who visit this intriguing area for the first time. After the Battle of Albert (22nd August) the fighting quickly extended eastwards and therefore, in the vicinity of the old 1916 battlefield and further east, there are numerous shared cemeteries where many men, killed during the late August - early September fighting are buried alongside their 1916 counterparts. For example, at the vast Caterpillar Valley Cemetery near to Longueval, the overwhelming numbers of graves date from 1916, but a small cluster of 24 graves mark the original establishment of the cemetery in August 1918 by the 38th Division. By contrast Lancashire Dump within Aveluy Wood has the reverse history - started in June 1916 and extensively added to during 1918.

In this chapter I have grouped the cemeteries and memorials into logical clusters, sometimes within the confines of an associated village or hamlet. Those groupings are as follows:

Section 1) *The valley of the River Ancre, south west of the town of Albert.*
- Bonnay.
- Buire sur l'Ancre.
- Dernancourt, including the communal and communal extension cemeteries.
- Heilly Station.
- Meaulte including Meaulte Military Cemetery.
- Mericourt l'Abbe.
- Ribemont.
- Ville-sur-Ancre.

Section 2) *The valley of the River Somme.*
- Bray-sur-Somme including Bray Hill and Bray Vale.
- 58th (London) Division memorial at Chipilly.
- Chipilly.
- Corbie, at the confluence of the Somme and the Ancre rivers. This also includes the suburbs of La Neuville and Aubigny.

Section 3) *The Morlancourt ridge area.*
- Beacon Cemetery.
- Dive Copse Cemetery.
- Grove Town cemetery.
- 3rd Australian Division memorial on the Bray - Corbie road north of Sailly le Sec.
- Morlancourt including the No 1 and No 2 British cemeteries.

Section 4) *The uplands west of Albert and the River Hallue valley. This area has so many cemeteries within that I have selected a small cross section in which interest relating to 1918 is abundant.*

- Acheux British Cemetery.
- Bavelincourt Communal Cemetery.
- Bouzincourt Ridge British Military.
- Contay British Cemetery.
- Franvillers Communal Cemetery Extension.
- Harponville Communal Cemetery and Extension.
- Hedauville Communal Cemetery Extension.
- Senlis le Sec Communal Cemetery Extension.
- Querrieu.

Section 5) *Others:*
- Bronfay Farm, south of Mametz.
- 18th Division memorial at Trones Wood.
- Mailly Maillet.
- Morval British Cemetery.
- The Rancourt area.
- Rocquigny-Equancourt Road Cemetery and Five Points Cemetery.
- Villers-Bretonneux and Fouilloy. This location is especially important in that many 1918 graves from the area covered by this guide were removed, after the war, to the Villers-Bretonneux cemetery.

118

Section 1) The valley of the River Ancre, south west of the town of Albert.

Bonnay.

This village lies just to the north-east of Corbie and can be easily reached along the D52 running from Albert past Dernancourt and Heilly. The military extension to the communal cemetery was used between April and late August 1918. As with many of the cemeteries in this area the April 1918 graves, almost all of which are those of Australian soldiers, relate to the fighting when the German spring advances were halted in the Villers Bretonneux and Dernancourt areas, whilst the later graves date from the Battles of Amiens and Albert. Amongst that latter group there are 24 graves of men who belonged to the 47th (London) Division. During the spring and summer of 1918 many of the British heavy artillery units were located along the road running north between Bonnay, Franvillers and Warloy-Baillon.

Bonnay Communal Cemetery Extension.

Buire-sur-l'Ancre.

Buire sur l'Ancre is another tiny hamlet alongside the Ancre. Like Bonnay, Buire can be reached from the D 52 past Dernancourt. Whilst passing this way you might like to stop to visit the graves within the communal cemetery. The six graves are all that is left of what was once a very busy and significant railhead area. During 1916 Buire was

119

The railway station in Buire sur l'Ancre, sketched in August 1918 by a member of 309 Siege Battery. The battery was one of many brought to this area to support the advance of infantry units during the second day of the Battle of Amiens - 9th August 1918. 309 Battery were located either side of the D52 in the chalk pits at the eastern end of the village. The station was a few yards to the south. [London Gunners. Ch XIII.]

thronged with British troops leaving for the UK, the vast majority on ambulance trains, the more fortunate on leave during quiet periods. Five of the graves date from 1916, just one from 1918. *(Map - Tour 2a)*

Dernancourt.

Dernancourt village lies south-west of Albert in the Ancre valley. The communal cemetery in Dernancourt can be easily reached from Albert, along the D52 Corbie road. That road passes through the village of Dernancourt and then passes under the railway bridge. Ignore the road leading back immediately on your right, which is parallel to the railway, but take the next small road after a few further yards, leading away on the right of the road towards the entrance to the communal cemetery, through which the Military Extension can also be reached. During the spring fighting of 1918 the 35th Division was forced back to the railway line here in Dernancourt with the large 1916 cemetery immediately behind their front line positions. By this time the German troops had taken control of the villages of Meaulte and Morlancourt as well as the higher ground of the ridge between these two villages. The 35th Division's men therefore had a very hard task in stemming the German advance at this position, which was completely overlooked from the south and south-east. *(Map - Tour 3c)*

Dernancourt Communal Cemetery Extension.

The finished appearance of this very large cemetery was created by the architect Edwin Lutyens. The two registers record 2,131 burials within the military extension. That extension had been started in

August 1916 after the arrival of XV Corps' Main Dressing Station here. That MDS operated by XV Corps was located along the right bank of the Ancre, on the expanse of open ground between the railway line and the river south-west of the village. Because of the location's long standing links with the RAMC's medical services a significant number of the men buried here are described as having Died of Wounds. Medical units, including a succession of CCSs, clustered in the vicinity until 26th March 1918 when Dernancourt was evacuated by the British forces. To bury the fatalities incurred at that time a small cemetery, known as Moor Cemetery, Edgehill, was used about half a mile to the west. After the war the graves of the 42 soldiers buried at Edgehill between the 23rd and the 25th March, 1918, were concentrated into Dernancourt extension. During the period April to August 1918 a further cemetery was created at Buire-sur-l'Ancre, almost two miles to the west, and after the war the graves of the 65 soldiers buried there were also concentrated into Dernancourt extension. The village of Dernancourt was recaptured on 9th August that year, by the 12th Division and the 33rd American Division. In September the cemetery was again used for burials. Although the great majority of the men buried here came from the UK there are 418 Australian soldiers, 51 from New Zealand, 33

One of the entrance porticos at Dernancourt communal cemetery extension.

Dernancourt communal cemetery extension with the original communal cemetery beyond.

from South Africa, 8 from Canada, 1 from India and 1 from the British West Indies as well as a number of Indian and Chinese Labour Corps members and 3 German prisoners. One hundred and eighty graves are unknown and there are a number of special memorials to men believed or known to be buried here.

The extension was built on the northern end of the communal cemetery which was used for burials between September 1915 and August 1916, and again during the retreat of March 1918.

Heilly.

Heilly can also be found by following the Ancre valley along the D52 from Albert, passing through Dernancourt and Buire-sur-l'Ancre before reaching Heilly village. Within the village the churchyard contains the graves of two soldiers, one a Liverpool Pal who died in the spring of 1916, the other a gunner killed in April 1918. However, by far the most significant cemetery in the area is located south of the village, across the Ancre, on the lower slopes of the Morlancourt ridge beyond the site of the railway station. *(Map - Tour 2b)*

Heilly Station Cemetery.

This is a very important location. To find it pass to the west side of Heilly towards Corbie and then take a left turn which leads south across the marshy and wooded floor of the Ancre valley. Continue for some way before crossing the Amiens - Albert railway line. The cemetery is immediately in front of you on the lower slopes of the

Apart from the unique arrangement of many regimental badges which it proved impossible to carve upon the close packed 1916 graves the cemetery at Heilly Station also houses a unique single grave, that of Lance Corporal J.P.O'Neill who had been killed, during January 1917, by the accidental detonation of a grenade. The marble column which marks his grave was erected by comrades who were indifferent to the regulations governing the uniformity of grave markers. Although appealing in its defiance of those regulations the question it poses is, of course, what would these cemeteries look like if many other examples of individual memorials had been allowed to remain?

ridge. An alternative and picturesque route is to follow the Ancre valley on its southern bank. Take the D42 from Albert towards Meaulte and there take the signs for Ville sur Ancre along the D120, thence into Treux and Mericourt l'Abbe. From Mericourt follow the Corbie signs and you will see the Heilly Station cemetery on the slopes after two kilometres.

There are almost 3,000 war graves here, 2,354 of which are those of soldiers and airmen from the UK. The cemetery also includes the graves of 83 men who were German prisoners of war. The bulk of the graves date from the summer of 1916 when this area was the scene of desperate and often futile attempts to deal with the overwhelming number of severely wounded men who were sent back to the three Casualty Clearing Stations which operated here, the 36th CCS, the 38th and the 2/2nd London CCS. During the period March-May 1918 it was used by Australian and British units and later for the burial of further hospital cases. The cemetery's appearance is unique in that the confined nature of many of the 1916 burials has enforced a situation where many headstones proved unable to carry all the regimental details. Consequently those regimental badges which proved impossible to carve on the headstones are placed on a covered wall which is found on your left as you enter the cemetery. The graves dating from the late summer of 1918 are in Plot VII, adjacent to the Great Cross at the far side of the cemetery from the entrance.

The cemetery is close to the location where Baron von Richtoven was killed when his plane was shot down and crashed into the hillside above and to the south of the cemetery on 21 April 1918.

Meaulte Village.

If you are travelling from Albert take the D42 Meaulte - Morlancourt road and turn left onto the main street which runs the length of Meaulte village. Shortly afterwards turn right, following the CWGC sign, along the minor road leading in the direction of Etinehem where you will find the Military Cemetery, 500 yards south of Meaulte, on the right hand side of the road. *(Map - Tour 3c)*

Meaulte Military Cemetery.

The cemetery contains almost three hundred graves, twenty one of which are unknown. There is a special memorial within the cemetery to eleven UK soldiers believed to be buried within the cemetery confines. After the war two significant nearby cemeteries were concentrated into Meaulte Military Cemetery. The first was Sandpit

Meaulte Military Cemetery.

Cemetery, which was located east of Meaulte at E.18.d.3,3. Also brought here were the graves from Meaulte Triangle Cemetery which was in E22, between the village and the light railway crossing on the Morlancourt road.

The village of Meaulte was occupied by British troops, who lived rather uneasily alongside three quarters of its pre-war population, between 1915 and 26th March 1918. On that date the village was evacuated after a rearguard fight involving the 9th (Scottish) Division. Meaulte was re-captured on 22nd August 1918, by soldiers serving with the 12th (Eastern) Division. As a consequence, apart from the 1915-16 graves, there are many graves dating from the third week in August 1918. Meaulte Military Cemetery therefore reveals a very accurate chronology of the British part in the fighting on the Somme during the Great War.

Mericourt l'Abbe.

This is an unusual and relatively large cemetery in being an eclectic mixture of men, drawn from many units, who died both in 1916 and 1918. After the Somme was taken over by the British forces in the summer of 1915 Mericourt-Ribemont Station became a railhead. The Extension was begun in August, 1915. It was used, chiefly by Field Ambulances, until July, 1916 after which it was closed until March, 1918. From March, 1918, to August, 1918, it was used by units engaged in the Defence of Amiens. The burials are within an extension to the communal cemetery and include a number of men killed during the August - September period of 1918. The bulk of these 1918 casualties are Australians soldiers. There are, unusually in this area, a

The cemetery at Mericourt l'Abbe. In the foreground are a group of German graves revealing the pattern of gaps where remains have been exhumed and removed. The cemetery contains the graves of many 18 year old soldiers.

substantial number of unidentified soldiers buried here - the result of battlefield clearances carried out after the war to the north-east of Mericourt along the Ancre valley. The CWGC details include reference to 11 German soldiers, four of whom died during 1919. From the headstones it is clear that 6 of these graves have been removed.

Ribemont.

This is an important cemetery in relation to the fighting during 1918. Burials did not begin in this location until the March of 1918. Initial internments were in the south corner of the communal cemetery but after July the extension was opened and following the end of hostilities many further graves were concentrated into the Ribemont extension from outlying parts of the 1918 battlefields. A number of smaller cemeteries were also brought into Ribemont including:

- Heilly British cemetery No.2. This was originally comprised of more than 100 graves within the grounds of Heilly Chateau, the imposing outer walls of which still stand today. It seems unusual that such a large and 'viable' cemetery should have been removed from its original context. I imagine that the fact that those graves were within a substantial and imposing private property will have had a bearing on the decision. The soldiers buried there were all killed during the period April-August 1918.
- Henencourt Wood cemetery. Again a viable cemetery, this was originally located half a mile to the west of the Henencourt

125

The important Ribemont Communal Cemetery extension which lies on a pleasant hillside site in the Ancre valley. *

village within the woodlands. This cemetery was in use between June 1916 and August 1918 and contained, by the war's end, more than 100 graves.

• Henencourt communal cemetery which contained 35 graves from the 1918 fighting.

• Point 106 British cemetery, near to the village of Bresle, which contained the graves of 25 men killed during March-May 1918.

The outcome of these concentrations was a cemetery whose register now records 482 burials. Within the cemetery there are 15 special headstones which record the burials of men in both Henencourt Wood cemetery and Point 106 whose graves were destroyed in later battles. *(Map - Tour 2b)*

Ville-sur-Ancre. The communal cemetery and military extension.

The original communal cemetery was enlarged by the addition of a number of British and Empire graves, the bulk of which date from the first half of 1916, amongst whom are ten men who served with the 97th Field Company, Royal Engineers, who were killed in action on 26th June 1916. During the German 1918 spring offensive Ville-sur-Ancre marked the point at which the British Army was able to re-establish a line south-west of the 1916 Somme battlefield and halt the German advance towards Amiens; a well preserved demarcation stone still stands at the junction of the D120 and the Morlancourt road just east of Ville-sur-Ancre. The British division in the area at that time, the week prior to 28th March 1918, was the 35th Division, one which had been at its establishment a bantam unit. After the retreat to the Ancre and its engagement in the Dernancourt, Ville-sur-Ancre and Treux sector the 35th Division was replaced by the Australian 3rd and 4th Divisions whose positions were extended to incorporate the 35th Division's lines. During the previous week the 35th Division suffered 90 officer casualties and 1450 amongst the other ranks.[1]

The military extension lies to the south of the communal cemetery. These can be found just west of the village along the D120 in the direction of Treux. The bulk of the graves are of men killed during the period 7th - 12th August 1918 during the Battle of Amiens. As is the case at Morlancourt British Cemetery Number 2, the Ville-sur-Ancre cemetery contains the graves of an extraordinarily high proportion of 18 and 19 year old soldiers, the men of 18 of 1918. *(Map - Tour 2a)*

SECTION 2) THE VALLEY OF THE RIVER SOMME.

Bray-sur-Somme.

Bray lies five miles south-east of Albert on the north bank of the river. The most direct route to Bray from Albert is past Meaulte and south east along the D329.

As was the case of the villages within the confines of the Ancre valley south west of Albert, the town of Bray's history during the Great War is one of extensive involvement in the treatment, evacuation and burial of casualties. Consequently there are a number of cemeteries here, including Bray British Military Cemetery to the north, Bray German Military Cemetery west of the town, as well as a French

The village of Bray sur Somme.

The Spartan brevity of the German military cemetery, to the west of Bray, contrasts with the open and pleasing aspect of the French National cemetery which is maintained in pristine condition on the north-western outskirts of Bray village.

National Cemetery, which contains the grave of one British soldier, and a Communal Cemetery which contains the graves of three further British soldiers. The town was closely associated with the evacuation of casualties from XIII Corps' sphere of operations, east of Mametz, during the earliest days of the Battle of the Somme. During September's fighting the ground adjacent to the British Military Cemetery at Bray was used by the Main Dressing Station of XIV

Corps. During 1917 the town was used by the 5th, 38th and 48th Casualty Clearing Stations and the overwhelming majority of burials within Bray British Military Cemetery date from 1917. Bray was captured by the Germans in March 1918 and recaptured by the 40th Australian battalion on 24 August of that year. There are a number of late 1918 burials within this cemetery, both of Australian soldiers and men serving with the 47th Division. However, just outside the town are two smaller British Military cemeteries, both of great interest to us in our journey around the battlefields fought over in late 1918.

Bray Vale cemetery is on the east side of the D329 Albert road at the southern end of Happy Valley and contains 281 graves, of which 172 are unknown. A very considerable number of the known graves record men who served with the 47th (2nd London) Division and who were fighting towards Happy Valley on the morning of 22nd August

Looking across Bray Vale Cemetery into the confines of Happy Valley.

Looking down across Bray Vale Cemetery from the high ground astride the Etinehem to Meaulte road, south west of Bray Vale cemetery.

during the Battle of Albert. On IGN maps the valley is noted as 'Vallee du Bois Ricourt'. The cemetery was expanded in 1923 by the concentration here of a number of 1916 graves removed from the Thiepval and Courcelette areas.

Bray Hill cemetery lies on the west side of the D147 Bray to Fricourt road as you approach the plateau overlooking Happy Valley, which falls away to the west. Bray Hill cemetery contains the graves of 104 Allied soldiers, most of whom were killed during the period 22nd to the 26th August 1918.

Apart from being associated with the locations fought for by the soldiers of the 47th (2nd London) Division on 22nd August 1918 these cemeteries also contain the graves of a number of Australian soldiers serving with the 3rd Australian Division. The 3rd Australian Division was covering the right of the 47th Division's advance on 22nd August and were then involved in the fighting to capture Bray-sur-Somme on subsequent days. The cemetery on Bray Hill also contains the graves of a number of soldiers from the 58th Division. One particular place of interest adjacent to Bray Vale cemetery is the valley to the north, Happy Valley, which was the scene of the ill advised attack made by a squadron of the 1/1st Northumberland Hussars, on 22nd August 1918, who rode up the valley in an attempt to capture the high ground on its eastern side towards the site of Bray Hill cemetery and Chataigneraie Farm to the north. Here, as they topped the eastern sides of the valley the mounted soldiers were met by barbed wire entanglements, close range rifle and machine-gun fire as well as bombing from the air! The 23 surviving men were withdrawn to rally in the sunken lane, west of the valley's entrance, on the D329.

Chipilly.

This is the site of a very distinctive memorial to the soldiers of the 58th Division. The Londoners, Territorials, who formed the majority of the ranks within that division had effected a remarkable feat of arms in the capture of the village on 9 August. The twin villages of Chipilly and Cerisy face each other across the Somme beneath the Morlancourt ridge. There are a number of important French and British Military Cemeteries within Cerisy. Adjacent to the French National Cemetery are two plots of British graves of great interest to those of you interested in the events of July 1916 at La Boisselle and Thiepval.

The valley floor location is attractive and much frequented by anglers and holidaymakers who have built many precarious dwellings on the river banks. However, the best positions to seek out are those on the steep ridge north of Chipilly which quickly climbs towards Gressaire Wood. This ridge is marked on IGN maps as the 'Camp de Cesar' and it is quite clear from the surrounding earthworks that the location was indeed the site of Roman fortifications during Julius Ceasar's subjugation of the Gauls. The reasoning behind the camp's location is immediately apparent since the Chipilly ridge is surrounded by the Somme on three sides, forming something of a peninsula, whilst affording commanding views towards the west and Sailly Laurette along the Somme's valley and across the Petite Vallee towards Malard Wood, the Bois des Celestins and north towards Gressaire Wood.

Just north of the village is the communal cemetery and extension on the Etinehem road. The graves here date from 1915 and 1916. At the cemetery the road forks and it is interesting to take the smaller track to the left which leads along the contours on the western slope of the Chipilly ridge. This track, which after two kilometres eventually becomes very deeply rutted and only passable to four wheeled drive vehicles, eventually passes through Gressaire Wood before emerging above Etinehem village. Before you travel down in a car remember that the track which is composed of compacted chalk can be very slippery in wet weather. You have been warned! *(Maps - Tour 3a & Walk 2)*

There are very fine views to the west from this track. In order to help you understand the significance of these positions I have incorporated here some of the detail from Chapter 3 to help explain the events from the German perspective. On the first day of the Battle of Amiens, 8 August, this area was the scene of intense fighting which saw the soldiers of the 58th (London) Division engaged in an attempt to push the Germans from the Chipilly Ridge. The village of Sailly Laurette was quickly captured by the 2/10 Londons and the Germans were disappointed that their troops in that village had been taken by surprise. The next obvious point of resistance for the Germans was Malard Wood. However, by 9.30 am the 2/10th Londons were one thousand yards east of Sailly Laurette on the ridge between the village and Malard Wood, giving this unit a clear view of Chipilly to the east. Their advance had netted an arsenal of weaponry including 98 machine guns and 23 trench mortars as well as 285 prisoners! Malard Wood however was a much more difficult location to capture. The wood (and the adjacent Bois de Celestins) is clearly visible on the skyline to the west from the track on the Chipilly Ridge. In the fighting for this commanding position the Londons (6th, 7th and 8th Battalions, 174 Brigade) were hard pressed yet managed to capture the eastern perimeter of the wood by 8.00 am although many isolated groups of

Looking west from Chipilly Ridge in the direction of Bois Malard, beyond which the slopes above Sailly Laurette were captured by the 2/10th Londons on the morning of 8 August whilst the 3rd Australian division advanced on the right of the River Somme whose valley is to the left of the photograph.

German soldiers continued to resist within the confines of the woods until early afternoon.

From the Sailly Laurette to Morlancourt road and their positions in and just north of Malard Wood the London's machine gunners were able to train their guns on Chipilly village and a constant fire fight grew between the German machine gun teams dug in on Chipilly Ridge and the 58th Division's guns. However, whilst the German army maintained control of Gressaire Wood to the north of Chipilly Ridge they remained confident that their positions north of Chipilly village were secure. Since the final objectives allotted to the 58th Division had not been reached 173 Brigade was detailed to effect this final part of the advance. Following closely behind the soldiers of 174 Brigade 173's men passed through Malard Wood. As soon as the two assault battalions of 173 Brigade, the 3rd and 2/4th Londons, left the shelter of Malard Wood they were subjected to heavy and accurate machine gun fire from the slopes north of Chipilly, only a small number of men advancing further east towards the higher ground on the Chipilly ridge. From the track north of Chipilly it is easy to visualise the scene that morning. Belief that some British troops were holding Chipilly ridge caused much delay throughout the day. This was a real problem for the Australians on the south of the Somme who were taking many casualties from machine guns, in the village of Chipilly, firing in enfilade. Therefore the 2/2nd Londons were brought up from brigade reserve. After an initial delay, consequential upon concerns about the whereabouts of the most advanced British troops, the 2/2nd Londons advanced at 3.00 pm only to be met by a hail of machine gun fire from the front as well as from the north around Gressaire Wood and the south-east from the slopes above Chipilly. The battalion was forced to fall back into the shelter of Malard Wood.

Later that evening, at 7.30 pm, a further attempt to advance to the eastern side of the Chipilly spur was made by 175 Brigade and with the co-operation of 2/10th Londons who would advance from Sailly Laurette. However it was again very clear that the overwhelming strength of the German machine gun positions north of the village of Chipilly would prevent any advance. Some small groups from the 2/2nd Londons did get as far as the Morlancourt road, north of Chipilly, overlooking the valley, but were under such pressure that they were withdrawn at midnight.

The following day's attack was launched late at 4.15 pm. The 6th Londons of 174 Brigade attacked Chipilly in the face of severe enfilade fire from Les Celestins[2] as well as from the ridge above Chipilly. They were supported by the initiative of men belonging to the 2/10th Londons who had remained in the south east corner of Malard Wood overnight. The London's men then worked south-eastwards down the valley until they were forced to call for more artillery support to quell the machine gun fire from the German emplacements on the terraces just below the summit of the ridge. The 2/10th Londons entered the village under the protection of a smokescreen fired by the artillery. A line was secured, east of Chipilly and across the high ground north-east of the village, by 8.00 pm, enabling the soldiers of 173 Brigade to

The 58th (London) Division's memorial at the cross-roads within Chipilly. Nearby descriptions will give you an insight into the importance of the sculpture and the obvious expertise of its sculptor. I was a little saddened by the fact that the impact of acidic rainfall and the exposed position had begun, by 1997, to corrode some of this fine memorial's detail. However, the memorial has been well cared for by the village of Chipilly and it also now has the benefit of a Memorial Trust Fund dedicated to the future maintenance and preservation of this moving and important work. In 1998 renovation work was carried out and the memorial rededicated.

133

complete the capture of their objectives up to the south-eastern edge of Gressaire Wood.

Corbie.

Just outside the town is the remarkable Corbie Communal Cemetery and the Military Extension. This can be reached by following the Bray-sur-Somme road leading north from Corbie before taking the directions to the cemetery on the road towards Vaux-sur-Somme. The cemetery is one of the most visually appealing cemeteries, standing on high ground and approached by a sloping ramp. At the top of that ramp is located the grave of Billy Congreve, V.C., D.S.O., M.C. Congreve, who was the son of Lieutenant General Sir Walter Congreve, V.C., was killed in action during July 1916.

Corbie was, and remains, one of the most attractive towns on the Somme. It is located at the confluence of the River Somme with the smaller River Ancre. Corbie's ancient walls and many interesting buildings lend an aura of knowing antiquity to the place and many soldiers who trod its streets in the Great War years would have little difficulty in recognising its features were they to visit today. Perhaps they still do. During the great contests of 1916 this place was free from shellfire but in 1918 the town and the military cemetery was damaged by artillery fire. However, that impact was relatively small when compared with the utter destruction wrought on villages such as Thiepval or Combles in both 1916 and 1918. Today the scars of shell splinters can still be seen on the walls of a number of buildings and special memorials within the cemetery record those graves known to have been located here which were destroyed by German shellfire in 1918. *(Map - Tour 3b)*

In 1918 that German spring advance brought their armies to within 9 kilometres of the town. There were therefore no Casualty Clearing Stations in such advanced positions but Field Ambulances belonging to the 47th Division as well as the 12th Australian Field Ambulance were located nearby. The bulk of the 1918 graves are within Plot II, past the war stone at the northern end of the cemetery. Today Corbie boasts a very attractive town hall and the church is a fine building. Corbie is ideal for a lunch break away from studying and walking the 1918 battlefields and its many small shops sell a wonderful range of local produce, cheeses and fruit.

On the north side of the River Ancre in Corbie you will find La Neuville - where there is a Communal Cemetery Extension and the British Military Cemetery. The proximity of these two cemeteries to the Amiens railway line means that the vast majority of men here buried were wounded in early July 1916. Again, there are small numbers of casualties from the 1918 fighting in each cemetery. South of the River Somme in Corbie you will find Aubigny British Military Cemetery. This small cemetery contains the graves of many Australian casualties from 1918. The bulk of these date from the spring and summer but also record a number of casualties incurred during the August fighting. Apart from the 88 Australian soldiers there are seven gunners from the UK.

SECTION 3) THE MORLANCOURT RIDGE.

Beacon Cemetery.

This is the most central cemetery within the area described by this guide. The name Beacon Cemetery is derived from the 'Brick Beacon' which was sited on the highest ground of the Morlancourt ridge a few metres to the south-east. A briquetterie, facing the Bois des Tailles, was located some two kilometres to the east along the D1. The Beacon is an important cemetery in its own right, containing 768 burials, especially so in the context of this book in that the majority of the men commemorated and buried here were killed during the Battle of Amiens and the subsequent fighting for Morlancourt ridge. There are spectacular views to be had from the vicinity of the cemetery, only that to the south and south-east being slightly masked by marginally higher ground. However, this is one of the best places from which to visualise the fighting for the uplands between the rivers Somme and Ancre. The cemetery is best approached from the west along the D1 Corbie to Bray road having travelled past the 3rd Australian Division's memorial. From the low north wall of the cemetery you can look north-eastwards across Morlancourt towards Albert which can be seen clearly in the distance. Due east is the Bois des Tailles and Gressaire Wood. For the best views across the Somme valley I suggest that you walk a little south on the track which is close to the eastern boundary of the cemetery. *(Map - Walk 1)*

Beacon Cemetery.

During the spring of 1918 the German army's advance had taken their positions to the west of this location in a line running from Albert, past Dernancourt to Sailly-le-Sec. On 4th July those rather disadvantaged British positions were improved following an attack which brought the British front almost to Sailly Laurette, south of Beacon cemetery. On 8 August, the first day of the Battle of Amiens, Sailly Laurette and the Morlancourt road were taken by British troops belonging to the 58th (London) Division and the 18th (Eastern) Division respectively. Beacon Cemetery was first established by the 18th Division's burials officer on 15th August and the original battlefield cemetery, consisting of Plot III, rows C, E, G and I, comprised mainly of the graves of soldiers serving amongst the 12th Division whose attacks were to the north of the cemetery. I suggest this is a good place to read or re-read the details in Chapter 3 which deal with the events of 8/9 August in this area.

During the immediate post war years 660 outlying graves were brought in to Beacon Cemetery from small nearby burial sites. The difficult work of locating and identifying such burials accounts for the fact that there are 257 unnamed graves together with four special memorials to soldiers known or believed to be buried amongst them. Of the 768 burials recorded in the register 572 are those of soldiers and airmen from the UK. Amongst the larger of the outlying cemeteries concentrated into Beacon cemetery were:

• Croydon Cemetery, Glisy. This contained the graves of 27 UK and Australian soldiers who had been buried south of the Amiens to Villers Bretonneux road near to the Amiens aerodrome. It seems a strange decision to have brought these bodies of men killed during the period May to August, before the start of the Battle of Amiens, all the way to Beacon Cemetery, a site which is primarily concerned with casualties incurred during the days after 8 August 1918 during the Battle of Amiens proper.

• Sussex Cemetery at Sailly Laurette. This was located one kilometre east-south-east of Beacon Cemetery in the direction of Malard Wood. It was the site of 44 graves belonging to men killed on 8 August, the majority of whom were serving with the 7th Royal Sussex (18th Division).

• Taille Wood (Bois des Tailles) Cemetery. This was located just to the south of the Corbie - Bray road where it passes the wood and originally contained the graves of 16 Australian soldiers and two men from the UK killed during the period 13 - 23 August.

Storm clouds gather over Dive Copse cemetery. This is not a place to be in during severe weather. I speak from experience!

Dive Copse Cemetery.

This is not a place to stand alone on a cold winter's afternoon when dwindling daylight creates a sense of desolation and heartbreak which pervades this place. Yet, in summer the place is transformed by the heat of day and the ubiquitous skylark's song overhead. On such clear days the views south and along the ridge are very informative. The cemetery dates from the summer of 1916. Nearly 70% of the men buried here 'Died of Wounds' at the nearby dressing station in 1916. There are three rows of graves in Plot 3 from 1918 whose units reflect the divisions which fought here in August that year. There are 579 graves here in total. *(Map - Walk 1)*

Grove Town Cemetery.

Grove Town Cemetery is not a 1918 cemetery, but it is an extremely fine vantage point from which to gain an insight into the area attacked

Grove Town Cemetery, Meaulte. This cemetery, although consisting almost entirely of graves from 1916, is an exceptional point from which to view and understand the August 1918 fighting for the Morlancourt ridge. One grave which particularly caught my eye here, that of Private W.J.Barton, a 20 year old who died in 1916, was inscribed with words of great significance - 'Not my will, but thine be done.'[3] Such an expression of sentiment, which could easily be interpreted as opposing the war, is unusual. There are fine and almost uninterrupted views across much of the plateau. This is a place where a pair of binoculars and a compass would serve you well.

by the 12th (Eastern) Division during the August fighting of that year. There are extensive views in all directions including that northwards over Meaulte towards Albert and southwards across the Bois des Tailles in the direction of the River Somme. There are however very few graves within the cemetery from the 1918 period. Access to this area of commanding high ground is simple. Leave Meaulte on the D329 for Bray-sur-Somme. Past the entrance to the aerodrome, on your left, take the first right as you come onto the high ground of the Morlancourt Ridge. You will see the cemetery along a further track to the right. *(Map - Tour 3c)*

The Australian 3rd Division's memorial on the Bray - Corbie road.

The 3rd Australian Division's Memorial on the Corbie - Bray road.

At the start of the Battle of Amiens, 8 August 1918, the Australian Corps was located south of the River Somme. However, by the third day of that battle, 10 August, there were substantial changes in the organisation of Fourth Army units where the River Somme had not proved to be a good boundary between the Australian Corps and III Corps. It was decided to make the Bray - Corbie road into that boundary and the 3rd Australian Division took over the 58th Division's sector. This decision explains in part why the 3rd Australian Division's memorial is sited at the cross roads where the Sailly-le-Sec to Mericourt l'Abbe road crosses the D1. In my opinion it would have been far more appropriate to site the Australian memorial closer to Bray-sur-Somme where their men fought with distinction rather than on ground which had always been under the control of British units. *(Map - Tour 3b)*

Morlancourt.

This village can be reached on either the D42 road which runs south-west from Albert past the western end of Meaulte or via the D52 running through Dernancourt. Throughout the first three and a half years of war Morlancourt was a quiet location, much appreciated by the troops, who used its restful and plentiful supply of clean billets. The lie of the land meant that the village was sheltered from observation and was, in any case, beyond the range of German guns.

Throughout much of 1916 the place was the scene of operations for Field Ambulances. Morlancourt was captured by the German army in late March 1918 and recaptured by the British following the advances made during the Battle of Amiens. The capture of the Morlancourt area on 9 August by the 12th Division was undertaken by 37 Brigade. (See Chapter 3 and the section dealing with the events of 9 August.) This was the scene of the action where Sergeant Thomas Harris, Royal West Kent Regiment, won his posthumously awarded Victoria Cross. The actual capture of Morlancourt village was achieved by the 1/1st Cambridgeshires who were attached to 37 Brigade.

There are two British military cemeteries close by the village. Morlancourt British Cemetery Number 1 was made on the west side of the village by Field Ambulances, operating on the low ground in front of the cemetery during June and July 1916. This however is not a 1918 cemetery and our interest is focussed upon:

Morlancourt British Cemetery Number 2.

This cemetery lies next to the rough track leading back towards Ville-sur-Ancre. Unlike Morlancourt British Cemetery Number 1 the 56 graves in this cemetery were dug in August 1918 and the bulk of those graves belong to men who served within units of the 12th (Eastern) Division. As we have seen, Morlancourt village was re-captured on 9th August, the second day of the great offensive operation undertaken by Fourth Army known as the Battle of Amiens 1918. The cost of the subsequent advance on 22nd and 23rd August (the Battle of Albert) along the ridge to the east of Morlancourt towards Happy Valley and Bray is represented by a number of graves of men killed during those two days, at least 19 of whom were the 18 and 19 year olds upon whom the British divisions were by this time so dependant.[4] The cemetery is surrounded by a distinctive flint stone wall and access is gained across a small bridge which lends a very unusual and attractive aspect to the cemetery's appearance.

Morlancourt British Cemetery Number 2.

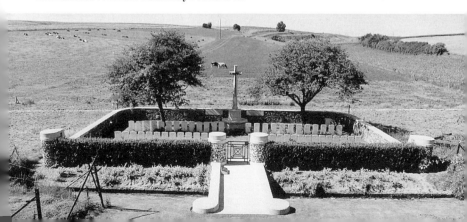

Section 4) The uplands west of Albert and the River Hallue valley.

Acheux British Cemetery.

The village is easily reached along the D938 from Albert, which also runs past Bouzincourt, Hedauville and Forceville with their own interesting history and cemeteries. The small cemetery here at Acheux is effectively two plots - one for 1916 and a larger group from 1918. If you have travelled out here from Albert it is only a short distance onwards to Louvencourt Military Cemetery, whose 1915-16 story is extraordinary[5] and also to the village of Varennes where there is a large British Military Cemetery which contains a considerable number of 1918 casualties.

Bavelincourt Communal Cemetery.

Bavelincourt lies in the valley of the River Hallue. Follow the D929 from Albert towards Amiens and turn right at Pont-Noyelles onto the D115. I would wager a fair sum that very few people who read this have ever been there. If that is the case I suggest a visit since the valley of the Hallue is rich in both 1916 and 1918 history. Supply units servicing the divisions fighting across the old 1916 battlefield during August 1918 trundled back and forth across this area's tiny lanes to railheads near Doullens. Where the river is bridged by the Albert - Amiens road south of Bavelincourt you will find the village of Querrieu with its chateau from where Rawlinson commanded the operations of so many Kitchener men during 1916. The River Hallue joins the Somme just after the Somme's confluence with the Ancre and

The remarkable Bavelincourt communal cemetery.

a little west of the town of Corbie. Bavelincourt's small 1918 cemetery has a link with the two London divisions which are frequently mentioned within this guide, the 47th and the 58th. If you travel across the river to the twin village on the western side, Montigny, you will find a similar cemetery with a similar background. Between them the cemeteries in Bavelincourt and Montigny contain fewer than 130 graves.

Bouzincourt Ridge Cemetery

This cemetery has very obvious links with the 1918 fighting in this area. The fact that it includes graves from 1916 suggests, on first sight, that the cemetery was begun during that period. However, the truth is that the graves of men killed before the autumn of 1918 have been concentrated into this cemetery from outlying burial plots after the war. The cemetery was constructed at the site of the German front line in the summer of 1918 (grid reference W.15.central). It is a magnificent viewpoint and one whose perspective over the 1918 fighting around Albert is unsurpassed. In the spring of 1918 the German advance was brought to a halt on this ridge by the 12th (Eastern) Division and the 38th (Welsh) Division. In August the 38th Division was here again and played an important role in pushing the Germans back eastwards. The original cluster of graves date from September 1918 and now form Plot I. After the war further graves were added, although some of these date from 1916 the bulk are from 1918. *(Map - Tour 1a)*

One grave of interest is that of Lieutenant Colonel J.S.Collings-Wells whose battalion fought here on 27th March. The men were tired and had suffered many casualties as they conducted a fighting retreat in the face of constant deep advances made by the Germans during the preceding week. The entry in the cemetery register record that Collings-Wells' men were ordered to undertake a counter attack just south of the cemetery's site and that he led the attack personally,

Bouzincourt Ridge Cemetery, the entrance of which mirrors the Thiepval memorial's arches. Bouzincourt ridge is a particularly fine vantage point from which to view the Thiepval positions.

though twice wounded, before being killed at the moment of achieving the objective.

Before the war the farm on the lane leading down into Albert was the site of another brickworks. The sunken nature of the lane there enabled the German troops to construct many protective dug-outs. British trenches west of the Brickworks were known as Torrens Trench and Torrens support. To the north, facing the cemetery, were Shell Hole, Welsh and Dragon trenches. Shell Hole trench gave some advantage to the British from its position straddling the very highest ground just west of the cemetery. This was captured during a subsidiary attack which took place at 7.30 pm on 22nd April, undertaken by the 113th Brigade and 2nd Royal Welsh Fusiliers of the 38th Division.

I should point out that this cemetery is not easily accessible by car in the wettest of weather. The track from the D20 is rough and deeply rutted by the wheels of tractors. However the sunken lane is interesting in that it was the British front line here in the summer of 1918. It was an uncomfortable place I imagine since it was easily enfiladed by rifle grenades from the German positions to the south-east adjacent to the cemetery! By the July of 1918 operational reports by the 47th Division pointed out that the Germans were increasingly dependent upon such small calibre projectiles[6]. To walk is the best advice that I can give unless you are certain of your vehicle's capacity to cope. I have already spent one happy hour digging a visitor's vehicle from the lane here!

Bouzincourt Ridge 1:5000 series trench map showing the area around the present site of Bouzincourt Ridge Cemetery. (W.15. central)

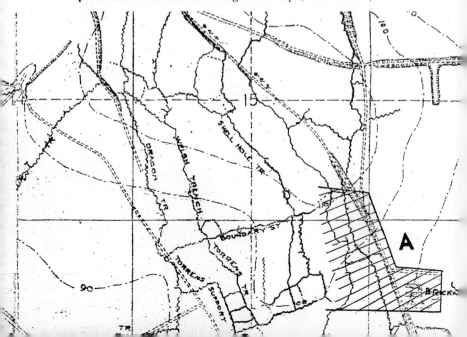

Contay British Cemetery.

This beautiful cemetery lies in the Hallue valley a little west of Warloy Baillon. There is a clear pattern to the 1916 burials and you will find a further 1918 plot, distinct from the rest of the cemetery, principally associated with the 38th (Welsh) Division. This is a very lovely location well worth seeking out.

Contay British Cemetery.

Franvillers.

The village of Franvillers stands north of the Ancre valley, and north-west of Heilly, close to the Albert - Amiens road. The communal cemetery extension was used between April and August 1918. The register records details of 248 British and Empire burials, 113 being of men from the UK and majority of the others from Australia. Almost all the graves relate to the early summer of 1918 but there are a number of interesting graves from the August of 1918 as well, including a significant number from the two Eastern divisions which fought here, the 12th and 18th.

Harponville Communal Cemetery and Extension.

This cemetery and that at nearby Hedauville are similarly sized. Again this is a 1918 cemetery and the majority of the graves relate to men who were killed whilst serving with two divisions which figure largely in the story of August and September 1918 - the 38th (Welsh) and the 17th (Northern).

Harponville communal cemetery extension.

143

'One Ricard too far!' The reverse of this new CWGC sign correctly says: 'Hedauville Communal Cemetery Extension.' How strange that no-one noticed the error during its manufacture.

Hedauville Communal Cemetery Extension.

Found a little way to the north-west of Bouzincourt along the D938 this is another 1918 cemetery. There is a strong link with many of the artillery units which operated on this high ground west of Albert - sixty one such men being buried here amongst the 178 graves within the extension.

Senlis-le-Sec Communal Cemetery Extension.

Senlis is located just west of Bouzincourt and north of Henencourt. This is a small cemetery containing less than 100 graves which date from 1918. Begun by divisions which again figure largely in the story of August - September 1918, the 12th (Eastern) and 38th (Welsh) divisions whose front line units were west and north west of Albert in late March 1918 and onwards. The adjacent communal cemetery contains a remarkable catacomb whose structure was clearly utilised during 1918 by the British units in this area. The brickwork still carries

Senlis-le-Sec communal cemetery extension and what appears to be graffiti left by Allied troops in the entrance to the nearby catacomb.

a number of names and regimental numbers which appear to have been left by British troops who sheltered here.

Querrieu.

This is the site of the chateau from where Rawlinson commanded Fourth Army during the long summer and autumn of 1916. The location merits a visit to see this important place because of that significant 1916 connection.

The chateau is beautifully located adjacent to the River Hallue's sedate summer trickle near to where the river is bridged by the D929 Amiens road. However, the nearby cemetery is of special interest to people following the story of 1918 in that it is comprised of almost 200 casualties from 1918 including the grave of Lieutenant Christopher Bushell, VC, DSO. Bushell was killed in front of Morlancourt on 8th August - the first day of the Battle of Amiens. (See Chapter 3.)

The Amiens - Albert road. This sketch first appeared in London Gunners. The Story of the HAC Siege Battery in Action. Kingham. Methuen & Co. 1919. It shows the screens, suspended across the road in the Amiens area not far from Querrieu, whose purpose was to hide the passage of traffic from German observation.

Further north along this incomparably lovely valley are the villages of Montigny and Bavelincourt already mentioned. Beyond those places more 1918 casualties are also buried within the tranquil cemeteries at Frechencourt and Warloy-Baillon.

SECTION 5) OTHERS.

Bronfay Farm.

This farm lies in an interesting position close behind the southern arm of the 1916 British sector of the Somme battlefield. Many of the graves within relate to the Manchester Pals and other units of the 30th Division which was here during late 1915 through to the July of 1916 when the farm was XIV Corps' Main Dressing Station. However, there are a considerable number of 1918 graves - buried mainly in two long

Bronfay Farm cemetery.

rows at the rear of the cemetery. There are extensive views from here across The Loop and down towards Bray and west across parts of the Morlancourt Ridge.

Mailly Maillet.

There are considerable numbers of 1918 casualties buried within the villages of Mailly Maillet and nearby Engelbelmer. Among the 1918 graves within Mailly Wood Cemetery is that of Sergeant Harold Colley, VC, MM, 10th Lancashire Fusiliers, who died of wounds following actions at Martinpuich on 24th August by the 17th Division.

Sgt Harold Colley, VC, MM, 10th Lancashire Fusiliers.

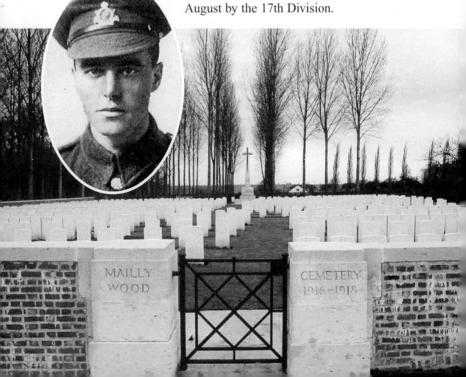

Morval British Cemetery.

This is a unique place. Although situated on the area of the 1916 battlefield it does not contain a 1916 casualty! The cemetery was constructed in order to bury 54 men of the 38th Welsh Division, although the cemetery also holds the grave of one German POW who died in September 1916. Morval village can be reached easily from Longueval at the centre of the 1916 area. Travel east through Ginchy and continue to Morval. The cemetery can be reached on foot from the centre of the village and is found along a path within a peaceful and rural setting. From here it is a short step to the Rancourt area through the village of Combles to the south of Morval.

Renovation works by a CWGC team in progress (March 2000) at Morval British Military Cemetery. I was rather uplifted by the sight of maintenance and renewal still continuing amongst these small and isolated cemeteries, more than eighty years on, and can only hope that the will to finance this process continues to flourish strongly in order to honour these men's sacrifice.

The Rancourt area.

The village of Rancourt lies to the east of the A1 motorway. Travel south from Morval along the D11E/D74 until you enter Combles. Within Combles are two cemeteries, although that which holds interest relating to 1918 is the Combles Communal Cemetery Extension on the north-east of the town. There are a number of original graves from 1918 as well as further graves concentrated here after the war. Leave Combles on the D20 in the direction of Rancourt. The village of Rancourt is the site of two massive cemeteries - Rancourt German and Rancourt French National. Together these two cemeteries contain almost 20,000 graves. Between the two you will find the comparatively tiny and far more intimate British Military Cemetery with its 92 graves. The greatest number of those graves are linked to the advance of the 47th (London) Division across this area in August and September of 1918. A short distance north of Rancourt you will also be able to find Sailly Saillisel British Military Cemetery. As at Rancourt you will notice many London unit graves here amongst more than 750 others which have been concentrated into this cemetery after the war.

Rancourt village where the small British Military Cemetery is overlooked and dwarfed in extent by the French National Cemetery to the east and by the German Military Cemetery to the west. The close proximity of cemeteries belonging to the three major combatants on this part of the Western Front is a striking and unique feature of Rancourt village.

Sailly Saillisel British Military Cemetery.

From Sailly-Saillisel you can drive to the Canal du Nord via Mesnil-en-Arrouaise and Manacourt. The canal is a formidable obstacle and its crossing at Etricourt, by the 38th Division and the 18th Division to the south, was a remarkable feat of skill, bravery and endurance by so many youthful soldiers.

Rocquigny - Equancourt Road Cemetery and Five Points Cemetery.

These two immensely interesting cemeteries lie at the eastern extremity of this guide, on the west side of the Canal du Nord between the villages of Etricourt and Ytres. If they are the last cemeteries which you visit after a long day in the field they will never cease to intrigue and interest you. I have to admit that these are some of the most telling

148

Five Points Cemetery.

The German headstones at Rocquigny - Equancourt Road Cemetery.

and interesting cemeteries which I have ever visited and the story which each revealed held my attention for many hours amidst their tranquil and infrequently visited surroundings.

The larger of the two is the Rocquigny - Etrancourt Road Cemetery whose register records 1,838 War Graves. There are 1,764 burials within this cemetery which includes the graves of ten French civilians as well as 66 German soldiers who were killed during the last three months of the war. Although the cemetery was begun in 1917, during the German Army's retreat to the Hindenburg positions, there are many plots relating to 1918's events.

The smaller cemetery is Five Points, just a few hundred metres to the north. This is, by contrast, an intimate battlefield cemetery, marked as distinctive by the use of red stone for the headstones. The cemetery includes the grave of Brigadier General A.R.C. Sanders, CMG, DSO and bar, the commanding officer of 50 Brigade, who was killed on 20 September 1918. In total this cemetery contains 101 graves, almost all of which are known.

Villers-Bretonneux.

The village is easily accessible from the vicinity of Corbie along the D23 which runs through Fouilloy. The fighting in 1918 affected Villers-Bretonneux greatly. It was captured by the Germans on 23rd April 1918 but the following day was recaptured by the 4th and 5th Australian Divisions as well as units from the British 8th and 18th Divisions. It was the launchpad for the Australian 2nd and 5th Divisions during their attacks on the first day of the Battle of Amiens (8th August 1918). The Villers Bretonneux Military Cemetery will be found on the high ground of a spur above the River Somme's south bank. It contains the graves of 1089 UK soldiers, 779 Australians, 267 Canadians, 4 South African and 2 New Zealand soldiers. The site is also the location of an important Australian National Memorial which will be of interest to all who visit this place.

The graves from a number of small cemeteries which would, had they been allowed to remain in situ, have fallen within this guide's confines were concentrated into Villers-Bretonneux. I therefore thought it appropriate to refer you to this important cemetery. The cemeteries of principal interest brought here to Villers-Bretonneux were:

• High Cemetery, Sailly-le-Sec. This originally contained eighteen UK and eleven Australian soldiers who were killed in the period June to August 1918.

• Kangaroo Cemetery, Sailly-le-Sec. Like High Cemetery this was located on the Sailly-le-Sec to Ville-sur-Ancre road. Kangaroo Cemetery contained the graves of 13 Australians killed during March-April of 1918 as well as the graves of 14 soldiers serving with the 58th (London) Division who were killed during August 1918.

• Vaux-sur-Somme Communal Cemetery and Extension. The Extension, made in May-August 1918 contained the graves of 130 Australians and 104 UK soldiers, mainly from the 58th Division.

1. See H.M.Davson, *History of the 35th Division in the Great War,* Sifton Praed & Co., London, 1926. There is a clear and informative account of the fighting for the defence of the Albert - Amiens railway line and the Ancre valley, by the 35th Division, on pages 205 - 217 inclusive.
2. Today the Bois de Celestins is effectively an eastern continuation of Malard Wood.
3. Also Jesus Christ's last words on the stake as he died.
4. In reality many more than the 19 which I have mentioned may have been 18 or 19 years of age since their ages are not mentioned upon their headstones or within the cemetery register entries.
5. First British officer to be killed on the Somme, Captain Rollaston; 2nd Lt Roland Leighton fiancee of Vera Brittain - Testament of Youth; Br.Gen Prowse - most senior 1st July 1916 casualty.
6. Public Records Office. WO95/2743. 47th Divisional Headquarters.

Chapter Six

THE TOURS AND WALKS

Tour One[1]

The British Positions west of Albert and north of the River Ancre.
This tour is ideal in summer on a cycle. It is not suitable for coaches or long vehicles at any time of the year. In winter the first part of the tour from Albert to Bouzincourt ridge is rather muddy and you should beware of difficult access to the cemetery astride that ridge. If you have access to a 1:20,000 series trench map of this area you will see how little the tracks and roads have changed since 1918 - indeed since before the start of the Great War. A suitable place to start this tour is at the bridge over the railway line to the north-east of Albert on the D50 Aveluy road. This railway line is the key to the understanding of the Albert area during the 1918 fighting. Whilst this railway line had been devastated by shellfire during the period 1915 to early 1917, the subsequent German withdrawal to the Hindenburg positions had enabled British engineers to reconstruct the track during 1917. Indeed the signal box adjacent to the bridge which crosses the railway on the road between Authuille and Mesnil still carries the date 1917. The loss of this part of the Amiens - Albert - Arras line to the German spring offensive had produced serious effects on the British Army's ability to undertake troop movements in the Arras to Amiens sectors.

This tour is aimed at making you familiar with the positions occupied by the British and Empire forces west of Albert and north of the Ancre after the German advance during the last week of March 1918. In the southern part of the area covered by this guide the foremost German positions after that advance ran from the banks of the Somme through the village of Sailly Laurette, thence northwards past the Brick Beacon on the summit of the Morlancourt ridge where the Germans had advanced their lines during 6th August, then northwards past the west of Morlancourt and down to Dernancourt in the Ancre valley. Parts of the village of Dernancourt lay in No Man's Land. From here the German positions turned briefly north-eastwards in the direction of Meaulte and Vivier Mill but again turned northwards past the western outskirts of Albert. From Albert those positions ran north across the Bouzincourt ridge adjacent to the British cemetery, thence through Aveluy Wood (marked as Bois d'Aveluy on your IGN maps) where many trenches from the period are still visible between the road and the railway line. Please take note that the wood is in constant use by hunting sportsmen and that traps are regularly set in the wood for deer and rabbits. You have been warned! North of Aveluy Wood the German 1918 spring advance took them into the village of Hamel on the banks of the River Ancre below Mesnil, thence up to Beaumont Hamel where their positions lay just east of the present day Newfoundland Park and thence on past the northern limit of this guide towards Bucquoy. In early August 1918 the Germans had made a tactical withdrawal from the Beaumont Hamel area so that, when the Battle of Albert began on 21st August, the German front line trenches

north of Aveluy ran east of the Ancre past Hamel and thence round to Beaucourt-sur-l'Ancre.

It was from the positions described above that Albert, and positions north in the direction of Thiepval, were attacked on 22nd August 1918, the opening day of the Battle of Albert proper, by the 18th Division through Albert and the 38th (Welsh) Division just to the north through the Aveluy area.

In order to start this tour you should consider two interesting alternative routes up to the Bouzincourt Ridge.

It is 22 August 1918 and men belonging to the RAMC and the 8th East Surrey Regiment, 18th Division, wait in readiness for action near Albert.

Firstly, in summer weather, from the bridge on the D50 take the road running west along the north side of the station sidings. You will quickly come to a cross roads where you can turn right, up the slope within a slightly sunken lane. After one kilometre take the left fork and this lane leads to the British military cemetery astride the Bouzincourt ridge. During the spring and summer of 1918 the German front lines ran across the high ground here before running north-eastwards across the D20 Bouzincourt - Aveluy road and the D129 Aveluy - Martinsart road before entering the southern end of Aveluy Wood. Take note that the track running past Bouzincourt Ridge cemetery is very wet in winter and you would be well advised if you find yourself here in such conditions to take the right fork which will bring you onto the Aveluy to Bouzincourt road, the D20, at which turn left for 800 metres after which you can easily walk back to Bouzincourt Ridge cemetery. From the cemetery there are extensive panoramic views across the Ancre valley north of Albert, towards Thiepval to the north-east and across the 1916 battlefield towards Pozieres and Montauban.

As a second alternative, in inclement weather and after heavy rain, from Albert travel to Aveluy along the D50. In Aveluy turn left and travel up the slope of the D20 for one and a half kilometres until you can follow the track towards the Bouzincourt Military cemetery on your left.

Tour1a.

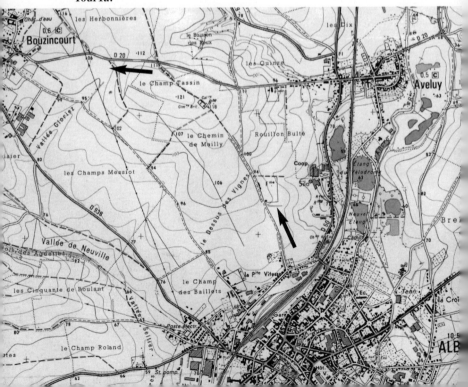

The cemetery was constructed on the site of the German front lines (grid reference W.15.central). Just to the west were a sequence of British front line, support and reserve trenches called Welsh, Dragon, Adelaide and Bouzincourt trenches. The names Welsh and Dragon are clearly associated with the 38th Division's tenure of this area during April and May when a number of localised actions and raids were undertaken with the intention of recapturing the highest ground here and providing observation into the Ancre Valley. The most significant of those actions here took place at 7.30 pm on 22nd April and was undertaken by the 113th Brigade and 2nd Royal Welsh Fusiliers.

Leave the Bouzincourt Ridge cemetery and head north-westwards towards the D20. During the summer of 1918 the British made use of the sunken lane here, and to the north of the D20, as their front line position. At the junction with the D20 (ref W.15.a.4.8) turn left towards Bouzincourt. There is a substantial British cemetery on the north west of the village, but that is associated with the 1916 period. Take the lane almost opposite the cemetery and travel south until you come to the D938. There turn right in the direction of Senlis-le-Sec which can be reached by turning left after one kilometre. All the villages in this area were troop billets in the 1915-16 period but the destruction of any remaining buildings was completed by further shellfire during 1918. There is a small 1918 cemetery in Senlis, most graves within which relate to the 38th (Welsh) and 12th (Eastern) divisions. There were few woods in this area within which to assemble concentrations of troops, the only one of substance was and is that at Henencourt.

From Senlis take the D119 in the direction of Henencourt which has a splendid chateau and a number of interesting remnants from the Great War, the most impressive of which are four substantial pillboxes which were built by British engineers belonging to the 47th Division in the summer of 1918. Today there is no British Military cemetery in the

Henencourt Chateau today.

village although that was not always the case. During the war, half a mile west of the village, there was a sizeable military cemetery within the Bois de Henencourt. A number of the graves there were destroyed by shellfire in the 1918 period. Surviving graves were removed to Ribemont after the war.

Here it is essential to mention a diversion which it is possible to make from Henencourt. This will lead you down into the lovely valley of the River Hallue. IGN map 2308 ouest will help but the route is simply explained and followed. Take the D91 to Warloy Baillon. There is a very large cemetery here, full of both 1915-16 interest as well as a number of 1918 graves. From there continue westwards into the Hallue valley along the D919 to Contay and thence to Bavelincourt, Montigny, Frechencourt and Querrieu along the D115. Bavelincourt and Querrieu are mentioned in Chapter 5. If you have a couple of hours this detour is an evocative and tranquil journey into the depths of the British rear positions of both 1916 and 1918. You can return to Henencourt via the D929 Amiens - Albert road taking the signs marked Bresle and thence

Tour 1b.

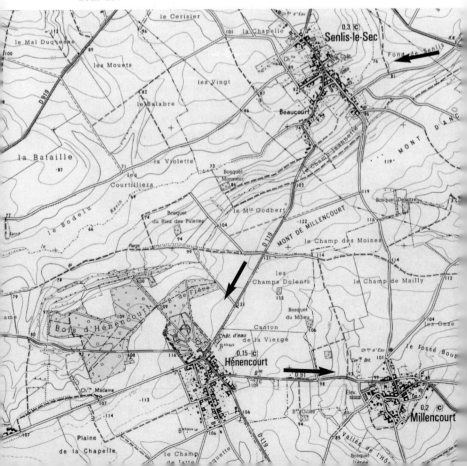

Henencourt, or alternatively proceed directly to Ribemont-sur-Ancre.

If you have not followed the diversion mentioned above, from Henencourt take the D91 to Millencourt, just outside which you will see the extension to the communal plot which is the British Military cemetery. Opposite the cemetery gates take the lane south in the direction of Lavieville and thence towards Ribemont-sur-Ancre, via the D119. The road from Lavieville to Ribemont crosses an area of broad upland and the Amiens to Albert road before beginning the descent into the Ancre valley whose low lying open spaces were a favourite target for German gas shells during the autumn of 1918. As you approach Ribemont you will be able to look across towards its large communal cemetery extension and this may prove to be an ideal moment to make a visit there. From Ribemont take the D52 towards Buire-sur-l'Ancre and from thence towards Dernancourt. During 1916 the open spaces alongside the Ancre were the site of extensive hospital and casualty evacuation facilities during the Battle of the Somme. Buire, and its twin village on the south of the Ancre, Ville sur Ancre, marked the British front lines during the summer of 1918. The British front lines were pressed forward to this location by the Australians who recaptured Ville-sur-Ancre, on the south side of the valley, on 18 May in a subsidiary action designed to improve the British position here in the valley floor. Before entering Dernancourt turn left before the railway bridge and head up the slope, keeping the communal and military extensions on your left. These places were where the 35th Division had halted the German advance just north of Dernancourt in the spring of 1918 and were therefore British front line positions during the summer. This lane will take you up a slope and back onto the higher ground across which the Albert to Amiens road runs. Travel for one kilometre past the large Dernancourt British Military cemetery until you pass a small copse on your right hand side. If you want to access the site known as the Grandstand this is an ideal opportunity - take the right turn soon after the copse (see Chapter 1).

Proceed across the plateau of high ground to the D929 Albert to Amiens road. Turn right onto the road in the direction of Albert. Within a few yards you will come to the summit of the plateau on its eastern edge overlooking Albert. These positions were important artillery OPs during both the 1916 Battle of the Somme and the 1918 Battles of Amiens and Albert. West of here in 1918 were enormous concentrations of British artillery. From here it is only two kilometres back into Albert where you will come across the demarcation stone on the right adjacent to the Amiens - Albert - Arras railway line. The stone

Tour1c.

purports to demonstrate clearly how the German lines, running north from the Vivier Mill/Farm area between Meaulte and Dernancourt, crossed the Amiens - Albert - Arras railway line here before rising up the Bouzincourt ridge due north of here. In fact the most forward German positions were 500 metres west of the stone.

Tour Two.

The Ancre valley between Meaulte and Corbie.

This is an incredible valley. The course of the Ancre south-west of Albert has been packed with great historical significance. Situated at the Ancre's junction with the River Somme the town of Corbie is a beautiful location. Here there are many surviving pre war buildings and two magnificent churches which give ample flavour of what an idyllic setting this place must have been. To men whose experience of 1916 had been horrific and emotionally damaging the town of Corbie had a special tranquillity. Even during 1918, when the Germans succeeded in getting their artillery much further west to bring Corbie within range, the town remained relatively intact. I always remember speaking with one ex Manchester Pal about this town. He described its peaceful ambience in endearing terms as he recalled how he had been hospitalised, with a serious ear infection, here in June 1916. After an operation and rehabilitation in 'Blighty' he discovered, on his return to

France by the early winter of 1916-17, that his unit, the 18th Manchesters, had been decimated at Carnoy. He never forgave himself for not having been with his 'Pals' on the 1st July 1916.

We know that the valley was home to the many medical units whose caring personnel saw to the needs of the tragic torrent of cases which populated this place in 1916. The numerous cemeteries

Just one of the many pre-war buildings which add enormously to the sense of atmosphere and period which can be felt in Corbie.

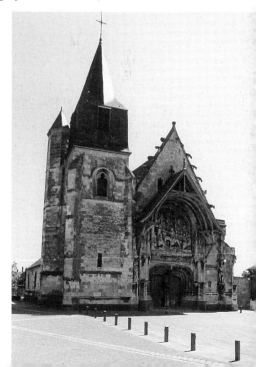

here, the most moving of which is undoubtedly Heilly Station, bear silent witness to the wretched squandering of life which the 1916 Battle of the Somme was. Hundreds of ambulance trains left here with their thousands of devastated, maimed and torn victims. The story has lent a permanent atmosphere whose presence can still be discerned as you look across the valley of the Ancre. It is not difficult to imagine in your mind's eye the flickering ruddy glare from the fireboxes and footplates as the locomotives idled at night; the calm efforts of medical personnel striving to fill the waiting carriages with their weeping, haggard and morphia ridden charges; the slow hissing and grunting of the engines; all conducted to the steady drum of shellfire to the east of Albert and witnessed by the teams of gravediggers labouring on the slopes above.

But within the context of this guidebook the Ancre valley is also home to the story of 1918, a narrative which can be followed along the course of two roads which define the north and south sides of the valley, the D52 and the D120. In summer this could be the basis of a leisurely ride on a bicycle, or for the more ambitious a two day walk with an overnight stay in one of Corbie's hotels. Even by car this evocative journey through time could not be conducted in anything less than three hours if you care to stop off at the many cemeteries and places of interest which abound within the valley.

The centre of Albert provides a sensible starting point. Leave the town on the Amiens road, the D929, then turn left onto the D52 in the direction of Dernancourt. This road almost exactly marks the course of the German front lines as they existed between the end of March 1918

Tour 2a.

and the start of the Battle of Albert on 21st August that year. As you enter Dernancourt village Vivier Farm is on your left, looking east towards Meaulte. This area was home to massive railway sidings and the start of the rail network which ran up onto the Morlancourt plateau. These sidings had been considerably extended during 1917. The loss of Vivier Farm and its sidings and facilities in the spring of 1918 was a disaster for the British transport system in France. Pass westwards through Dernancourt, under the railway bridge and along the flat low ground leading towards Buire-sur-l'Ancre. Half way there you will see an interesting French memorial on you right. As you approach that memorial you are passing across the British front lines which were pressed forward to this location by the Australians who recaptured Ville-sur-Ancre, on the south side of the valley, on 18 May in a subsidiary action designed to improve the British position here in the valley floor.

Prior to that Australian success, the next village you will come to, Buire-sur-l'Ancre, was the British front line during the spring of 1918. By the 2nd day of the Battle of Amiens, 9th August, 309 Siege Battery's guns and the jubilant gunners were brought forward to the two chalk pits at the eastern end of the village. The houses and church were in ruins, the debris of war abounded but the position in the chalk

The church in Buire sur l'Ancre, 14 June, 1918.

Tour 2b.

pits was a secure one. The chalky ground took the spade of the 9.5'
gun's trail well. 309's guns were engaged in counter battery work
against the increasingly hard pressed German units in the Becourt -
Fricourt area. The unit's chronicler recounted how:

> *'We enjoyed at Buire what was lacking in many other
> positions - a good water supply, and doubly welcome was this in
> that hot existence amongst the chalk, where, every time we fired
> the gun, we were enveloped in a cloud of chalk dust. Water could
> be pumped out of a sap in the chalk-pit, or - drinking water this
> - obtained from a pump on the railway station on the edge of the
> pit. Very soon too we tracked out a swimming place; we crossed*

162

*the railway line and a marshy meadow, and came to our old
friend, the Ancre, a narrow, swift little stream, and it was a
decided pleasure to plunge into its keenly cold waters.*[2]

It's just a few yards to the Ancre - you might like to try its refreshing
and 'keenly cold waters' yourself in summer. From Buire continue
along the D52 until you come to Ribemont and then Heilly. The village
of Heilly is especially evocative of the Great War era since it was far
enough west of the German artillery positions to retain some vestiges
of its pre-war appearance. On the western side of the village are the
walls of a remarkable and quite enormous ancient chateau. This has
been a beautiful village whose systematic despoilation by the
combatants during the war seems to have defiled the place and left it
unable to regain its previous grand rural atmosphere.

From Heilly continue along the D52 in the direction of Corbie. The
next village is that of Bonnay where you should turn right at the cross
roads and thence next left in order to bring you past the Military
Cemetery north-west of the village. Passing the cemetery you continue
into Corbie past la Neuville. Corbie has a fine character and possesses
a series of decent shops where you can obtain the ingredients for a
wonderful lunch. Quite the best place to eat that lunch would be at the
Australian memorial outside Corbie on the Villers Bretonneux road. In
front of the memorial buildings and observation platform there are a
number of wooden seats whose purpose seems tailor made for lunch.
If you can get access to the observation platform then you should do
so since the view across the Morlancourt ridge is unrivalled.

After visiting Corbie leave on the D1 on the east side of the town.
This will begin to rise up the slopes which soon become the
Morlancourt ridge. Soon after leaving Corbie there are excellent views
up the Somme valley on your right towards Cerisy and Chipilly which
was the scene of fighting involving the 58th Division within III Corps
during the opening day of the Battle of Amiens, 8th August. That
London Division was to advance past Malard Wood and the southern
tip of Gressaire Wood towards the great meander in the Somme which
surrounds the village of Chipilly. As you look along the Somme's
course today you can look left and along the lower slopes of the
Morlancourt ridge on top of which the 18th Division would capture the
higher ground.

However, you should leave the D1 by taking the left fork onto the
D120 which slides onto the northern slopes of the ridge and back down
into the Ancre valley. The first village along the road is the picturesque
hamlet of Mericourt-l'Abbe. However, before you reach Mericourt it is

essential that you visit Heilly Station cemetery. This is an unforgettable location from which views across the Ancre valley towards Heilly are both tranquil and yet terribly evocative of the horrors which this location witnessed throughout the war. The story of the cemetery needs little if any explanation - the close packed headstones tell their sad story with no need for elaboration.

From Heilly Station cemetery it is a straight forward route back to Albert through the villages of Mericourt, Treux, Ville-sur-Ancre and Meaulte. In the Ancre valley only Treux does not have a cemetery containing casualties from the 1918 period. Outside Ville-sur-Ancre is the junction where a lane leads back on your right towards Morlancourt. There is a demarcation stone here at the opening into the Morlancourt valley re-entrant. This was where the railway leading up onto the ridge was routed from Vivier Farm and Mill sidings before it began the ascent to the plateau and Grove Town.

Tour Three

The Morlancourt Ridge.

This proved to be a difficult area across which to devise a suitable tour. However, the outcome is, I think, an innovative journey which will enable you to see this upland area in a new light. Most visitors approach the Morlancourt plateau from the north or west since they are travelling from Albert or Corbie. I suggest that you try a different approach by leaving Albert in the direction of Peronne until you reach Fricourt. There turn right onto the D47 to Bray. Thence past Bray and south across the Somme valley in the direction of Proyart. Before there turn right onto the D71 and keep the Somme embankment on your right past Mericourt-sur-Somme, Morcourt, Cerisy, Gailly, le Hamel and thence into Vaire-sous-Corbie. Throughout that journey you have extensive views across the villages on the north bank of the Somme and the Morlancourt ridge. Initially, during the first three days of the Battle of Amiens this river bank was the border between UK and Australian forces but that junction proved unsatisfactory. Although there are extensive cemeteries at Cerisy today you would have been able to see other cemeteries along the north bank of the Somme in Sailly-le-Sec and Vaux-sur-Somme in the early twenties. Those graves were later removed and the bodies re-interred at Villers Bretonneux where, although it is the Australian memorial, the numbers of dead from the UK far exceed the numbers from Australian forces. Along the

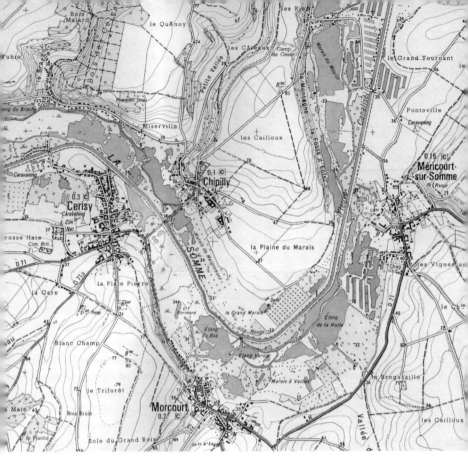

Tour3a.

way you will pass the site of the newly erected Australian memorial, at le Hamel, which has particularly extensive views across the southern aspect of the Morlancourt Ridge.

At Vaire re-cross the Somme and pass through Vaux, with its two multiple cross-roads, maintaining a north-easterly course uphill. One kilometre after crossing the Somme at the second cross roads junction keep the Calvary immediately on your left as you proceed further uphill onto the ridge until you reach the D1 road where you should turn right in the direction of Bray. At present you are behind the British front lines which existed here in the period April-August 8th 1918. However, as you look south-east towards the Somme you will be able to see the succession of steep sided valleys and woods towards Etinehem which made the German's defence of the ridge so tenable.

As you proceed along the D1 you will see the Australian 3rd Division's granite memorial obelisk on your left. This magnificent

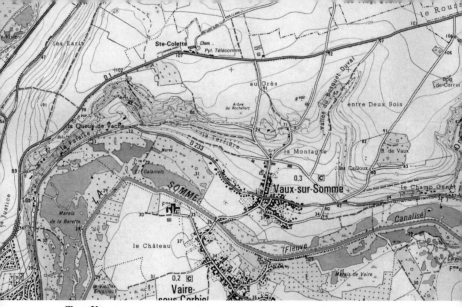

Tour3b.

stone is set at the junction with the Mericourt l'Abbe to Sailly-le-Sec road. Sailly, due south of here, was the foremost village in British possession before the attacks made by the 58th Division along the north banks of the Somme on the morning of 8th August. Proceed along the ridge, past the signs for Dive Copse cemetery which contains a number of graves from the August 1918 fighting, and on towards Beacon Cemetery. This is the location of the front line positions before 8th August, the German trenches running from the village of Sailly-Laurette to the south towards Morlancourt which is clearly visible to the north-east in its valley. Although the Australians appear to have 'bagged' the prime location for their 3rd Division's memorial the summit of this ridge was captured by the 18th Division during severe fighting. However the 18th Division's memorial, which commemorates their extraordinary and long lasting link with the Somme battlefield, is located at Trones Wood, west of Guillemont.

Past the cemetery take the first left towards Morlancourt on the D42. In Morlancourt you can visit the two small British Military Cemeteries there. Morlancourt was the scene of attacks made by the men of the 12th (Eastern) Division on the morning of 9th August, the second day of the Battle of Amiens. At the cross roads in the centre of the village turn back sharply right and then first left and then first right. That will return you to the D1 just west of the Bois des Tailles. To the west is the Briquetterie and to the south Gressaire Wood beyond which is Caesar's Camp on the summit of Chipilly Ridge where the 58th Division's men fought and below which is their fascinating

166

divisional memorial, within the village. This area north-west of Etinehem was also fought across on 9-10th August and American troops participated in the fighting for Gressaire Wood (again see Chapter 3). After 10th August the area south of the D1 Corbie - Bray road fell within the command of the Australian Corps to who the American 33rd Division were attached. Etinehem was captured by the 3rd Australian Division on 10th August.

Therefore, to complete our tour of the Morlancourt Ridge travel east along the D1 down into the valley between Tailles and Gressaire woods before turning left at the high ground near to the French National Cemetery above Etinehem. This was the site of the old Amiens Defence Lines which were located on the top of the east side of that valley (marked as Le Grand Riez on your IGN map) and were occupied by the Americans by mid-day on 10 August. Immediately after turning left off the D1 it is worth stopping to look down over Happy Valley and Bray Hill to the north-east, scene of attacks in that area by the 47th Division on 22nd August (see Chapter 4) during the Battle of Albert.

After one kilometre take the left fork in the direction of Meaulte. Continue across the high ground with the signs for Grove Town Cemetery on your right. As you approach the highest part of the ridge here you are coming to the best site to consider the events of 22 August, which witnessed a major initiative, by III Corps of Fourth Army, astride the Morlancourt ridge. The plan was to advance some two miles across a four mile width of frontage. Four battle weary divisions employing huge numbers of eighteen and nineteen year old soldiers were engaged in this attack. On your left, down in the low

The wreckage of Morlancourt village, 15 August, 1918.

Tour3c.

lying ground around Meaulte and Albert, the 18th Division were employed ensuring that Bellevue Farm and Vivier Mill were re-captured. On the right, to the south, the 3rd Australian division was to be used adjacent to the River Somme in an attack designed to push past the north of Bray-sur-Somme to their objective at the southern end of Happy Valley. It was anticipated that the ridge proper and the ground east of the Bois des Tailles would be captured by the 47th Division, on the right next to the Australians, and the 12th Division, on the left adjacent to the 18th Division. This advance would take the 47th Division's men past Grove Town cemetery which you can see clearly to the east.

To complete the tour continue downhill into Meaulte, past the Military Cemetery which contains many 1918 graves, and from there back into Albert.

Walk One.

Sailly Laurette in the Somme Valley to Beacon Cemetery on the Morlancourt Ridge summit.

Although this walk sounds strenuous it is in fact a pleasing stroll of just under seven kilometres (four and a half miles) which can be undertaken in two hours. A suitable place to start this walk is the church in Sailly Laurette which was located on the German front lines. Indeed, on the opening day of the Battle of Amiens it was two machine guns firing from the ruins of this church which caused many casualties amongst the 58th Division's men in this area. The village of Sailly Laurette faces the British front line village of Sailly le Sec across a steep valley which runs down from the Morlancourt spur into the Somme valley floor.

From the church the German lines ran up the spur above the village to the north-east along the course of the D42 Morlancourt road. As these German trenches approached the higher ground they were disadvantaged because the British troops had retained control of the highest ground here during the German Army's spring offensive. It was

Sailly Laurette, 8 August 1918.

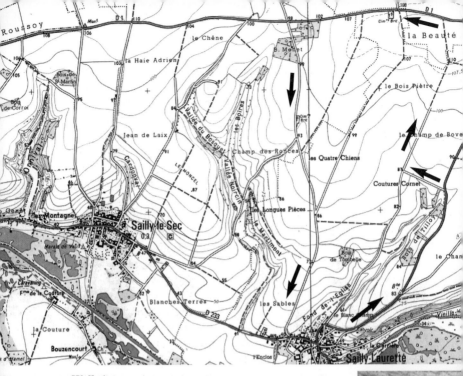

Walk 1.

a great surprise when, on 6th August 1918, the Germans pressed forward across the highest point on the summit of the Morlancourt Ridge at the site of the Brick Beacon thus condemning the first British attacks here on the morning of 8th August to be launched from inferior positions. As you walk up the D42 turn left past the small woods on your left and then right towards the summit. As you walk towards the higher ground there are extensive views south-west across the initial advance made by the 58th Division's men on the morning of 8 August.

At the summit you will be on the site of the Brick Beacon from which Beacon Cemetery has taken its name. Walk to the road, the D1, and turn left in the direction of Beacon Cemetery. That cemetery provides further very extensive views from its low northern wall across Morlancourt and beyond to Albert, whose buildings and spires are clearly visible in the Ancre valley, as well as to Thiepval on the far horizon. From here you can also look back

170

westwards to the Australian 3rd Division's memorial on the D1 in the direction of Corbie. This memorial marks the change in the organisation of Fourth Army units on 10th August caused by the fact that the River Somme had not proved to be a good boundary between the Australian Corps and III Corps. The D1 Bray - Corbie road was therefore made into that boundary explaining why the 3rd Australian Division's memorial is sited at the cross roads where the Sailly-le-Sec to Mericourt l'Abbe road crosses the D1. A far better location for the Australian would have been on the D1 north of Etinehem to demonstrate where the Australians took over the front lines after the advances to Chipilly by British Fourth Army units during the period 8th - 10th August.

Walk 200 metres past Beacon Cemetery on your left and take the first track on your left. As you progress you will see Dive Copse cemetery on you right as the slope begins to fall away down to Sailly Laurette. South of Dive Copse join the lane which runs down into Sailly Laurette. Here the British front lines faced east across the Fond de l'Eglise (Valley of the Church) in a position of parity with their German counterparts on the spur north-east of Sailly Laurette.

Sailly-le Sec, 8 August 1918. British artillery units move east in the direction of Sailly Laurette whilst captured prisoners move west towards Corbie and the POW cages. The Somme's waters can be seen behind the building. The scene is little changed eighty years on.

Walk Two.

Sailly Laurette in the Somme Valley to Cerisy, Chipilly, Malard Wood and return.

If you take the trouble to follow this walk you would find it almost impossible to believe that it had once been the scene of serious and devastating fighting amidst the torrent of events which marked the closing stages of the Great War. Apart from the cemeteries this area is seemingly unspoilt - a haven of tranquillity and glorious views and warmth in summer. This walk is approximately seven kilometres (four and a half miles) and can be completed comfortably within two hours. If you extend the walk onto the Chipilly Ridge, which I strongly recommend because of the wonderful panoramic views available from there, set aside a further one hour. The area is relatively sheltered and in the Cerisy - Chipilly area there are bars where refreshments can be purchased. As with many other Somme valley villages there are campsites along the course of this walk which would form an ideal base for visiting this area.

An appropriate place to begin is the church within the village of Sailly Laurette. This village was just behind the German front line in August 1918. On the opening day of the Battle of Amiens it was assaulted by the troops of the 58th (London) Division. Within minutes the village was captured by the 2/10 Londons (175 Brigade). You might like to refer to Chapter 3 for background to the events here. By 6.30 am on 8th August only two machine guns hidden in the wreckage of the church were still holding out, and those were dealt with by tanks allotted to this attack. Three hours later the 2/10th Londons were one thousand yards east of Sailly Laurette on the ridge between the village and Malard Wood, the Germans having fallen back to that wood and the adjacent Bois de Celestins.

From the church you can walk south across the Somme towards the hamlet of Gailly. The water course here is wide with a sequence of pools and woods either side of the causeway. This is fishing country and home to many holiday-makers in summer. In late April and early May 1917 Wilfred Owen, 2nd Manchesters and the war's greatest poet, was here suffering from 'neurasthenia'. Owen was treated at No 13 Casualty Clearing Station whose facilities were located adjacent to the canal lock. I think it worthwhile to refer you to another book in this series, Wilfred Owen[3], within which pages 60 - 66 deal interestingly with Owen's time here in Gailly. The final part of the water's course which you cross is the canalised section of the Somme, just before you enter the scattered houses of Gailly. Nearby is an attractive plinth, unveiled in 1998 by the villagers of Gailly, to the memory of Wilfred Owen. Here, on 8th August 1918, the Australians advancing across the open ground between le Hamel and Morcourt were taking heavy casualties from German machine guns still firing from the Bois de Celestins area to the north of the river. In Gailly, 100 metres after crossing the Somme, turn to the left and follow the lane eastwards in the direction of Cerisy and the two cemeteries which dominate the western approaches to that village. Although this location is, strictly speaking, outside the terms of this guide I think it relevant to give a little background to these cemeteries.

The Cerisy French National Cemetery is the first at which you will arrive. There are two plots of British graves containing almost 400 bodies, of which almost three hundred are unknown. The graves have been removed to here as a result of battlefield clearances. The greatest number come from La Boisselle but others are from Thiepval - both 1916. 1918 is represented by men who were killed during the German Spring Offensives as well as Australians from the August and

Walk 2.

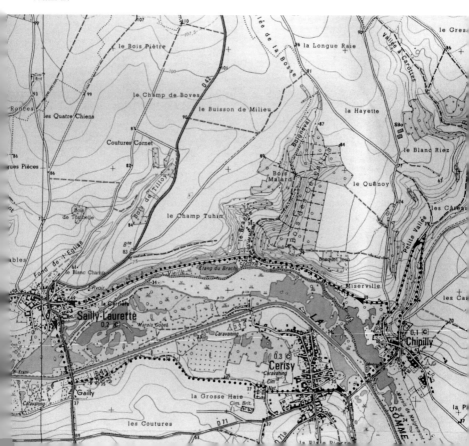

September of 1918. Just to the south is the British Cerisy - Gailly Military Cemetery which contains almost 750 graves. Apart from Canadians moved here from their sector of the Amiens battlefield, there are the 260 soldiers from a cemetery which once existed at Maricourt crossroads. I think it rather a sadness that these men's final repose is so far from the places where they sacrificed their lives.

From the locations of the cemeteries in Cerisy it is difficult to see across the Somme because of trees. However, if you walk past the French National Cemetery and through Cerisy village you can now re-cross the Somme under the lower slopes of Chipilly Ridge leading up to Caesar's Camp. This was the scene of great international co-operation between the 58th Division's men and small groups of Australians as well as American troops during the hours of 9th August as the village and the ridge above were captured that day. The village is home to the remarkable memorial to the 58th Division's men and this

Cerisy is a popular holiday destination within which a number of adjacent cemeteries are often overlooked by the many fishermen and picnickers who throng to this spot in summer.

is the ideal opportunity to visit it.

As you face the memorial and church you must decide how to return to Sailly Laurette. There are two alternatives:

Alternative one keeps to the valley floor. Turn left and walk westwards along the Somme valley floor. Initially the road swings northwards, right handed, around the lower slopes of Chipilly Ridge and you will enter the mouth of the Petite Vallee with the ridge above you to your right. Here the road forks - keep left and then, after 100 metres, turn sharp left towards Sailly Laurette. The road is roughly three kilometres of level flat stroll back to your starting point. After one kilometre you can see the Bois de Celestins on you right, to the north. Just past that wood a valley opens and you can stroll north into its confines past many holiday homes. The track takes you, if you want, up into the Bois de Celestins and Malard Wood[4]. This would be a good place to re-read the details of the 58th Division's exploits here on 8/9th of August 1918. From here it is an easy walk back to Sailly Laurette along the Somme valley floor.

Alternative two ascends the lower slopes of Chipilly Ridge. From the church in Chipilly walk uphill in the direction of Etinehem. After 200 metres you will come to the communal cemetery with its small extension, the graves within which are principally from the 1915-16 period. Opposite the cemetery a small lane forks off to the left and continues along the contours of the Chipilly Spur. Walking along this lane gives wonderful panoramic views across the Petite Vallee towards the Morlancourt Ridge. On the far side of the valley is the Bois de Celestins and to the north is Gressaire Wood. During the fighting here on 9th August the centre of III Corps' attack here was made by the enthusiastic soldiers of the Americans' 131st Regiment. From Malard Wood the 1st and 2nd Battalions with the 3rd Battalion in support deployed to face Gressaire Wood. As they moved between Malard and Gressaire woods, less than a mile in distance, the men began to suffer heavy casualties from machine gun fire emanating from Gressaire Wood and also in enfilade from the machine gun emplacements below the summit of Chipilly ridge. The crossing of the open ground between the two woods took almost two hours and had to be supported by a company of the 3rd Battalion as well as by the 7th Londons. By 8.00 pm the Americans were able to take their left objectives in the south west corner of Gressaire Wood. From your position here on the slopes of Chipilly Spur you can see how utterly exposed the Americans were to machine gun fire from these positions.

I suggest that, 500 metres after joining the chalk lane, you take the rough track which leads down into the Petite Vallee. In the valley turn sharp left and walk south back in the direction of the Somme until you reach the road between Chipilly and Sailly Laurette. There turn right and then, after 100 metres, turn sharp left towards Sailly Laurette. You are now back on the route described in 'Alternative one'.

Walk Three.

Aveluy, Bouzincourt Ridge, Martinsart and Mesnil and return via Aveluy Wood.

Well, this is one you could cheat on! You could do this on a bike, in a car or on foot. It is a simple circular walk of almost nine kilometres (five miles). But if you think that sounds a long way - just stop to think how those soldiers lumping a full pack of kit for miles as they trudged these chalky lanes in 1918 would have felt in the face of a mere stroll of five miles with no pack or stores to carry! On a summer's day this is great exercise with fantastic views. The walk mixes both 1916 and 1918 history in plentiful quantities. Two and a half hours is ample on foot. Half an hour by car.

Start within Aveluy and travel west along the D20 Bouzincourt road until you approach the high ground of Bouzincourt ridge. At the cross road 900 metres west of Aveluy turn right. Here you are just behind the German front lines. Their support line known as Rejection Support ran along the west lip of the sunken lane you have just turned onto. The British positions were astride the highest ground west of here and just west of Bouzincourt Ridge cemetery. Follow the sunken lane down to the D129 Martinsart road. There was a trench railway line running towards Mailly-Maillet in this valley throughout 1916 to 18. Turn left onto that road and continue along the valley until the land begins to rise past the unusual sight of the red headstones within the British military cemetery outside the village. The German spring advance had been stopped here at the foot of this slope. The German's front line trench, known here as Ragged Trench, ran into Aveluy Wood where it straggled in a north easterly direction through the wood in the direction of Hamel.

Unfortunately the confines of Aveluy Wood are not easily accessible. The wood is frequently used by trappers and hunters and may be dangerous to enter. During the spring of 1918 it was the Royal Naval Division's men who had halted the German advance at the north end of Aveluy Wood. Within the wood are numerous trenches in a remarkable state of preservation. However, you can walk to the west of

Aveluy Wood through the villages of Martinsart and Mesnil. Martinsart was a vital billet village for the 36th (Ulster) Division in 1916. Mesnil was the location of the 36th Divisions most important artillery OP known as Brock's Benefit.[5] The cemeteries within each village contain some 1918 burials.

Walk through Mesnil and turn down the slope facing Thiepval. Due east you can see the massive structure of the Thiepval Memorial to the Missing. Between lies the Ancre valley. In this area between Mesnil and Hamel many trenches, no longer visible, were hurriedly dug in the attempt to halt the German tide. They often had a naval flavour to their names; Hood, Hawke and Drake alleys amongst others. Walk downhill towards Authuille past Mesnil's rather eccentric chateau. After their arrival here in late March 1918, the Germans trenches, known as Casualty, Casualty Support and Reserve exited the northern end of Aveluy Wood towards the foot of this slope. From there the German lines had run north towards Newfoundland Park whilst their British counterparts ran towards Auchonvillers. Those German positions were therefore considerably disadvantaged in terms of both elevation and

Lancashire Dump cemetery - Aveluy Wood.

observation. In early August, before the Battle of Albert, those German lines were pulled back onto the east bank of the Ancre. It was here on 21st August that the 21st Division as part of V Corps opened the attempts to cross the Ancre in the Hamel - Beaucourt area. In the Hamel - Aveluy - Albert area it was the Welshmen of the 38th Division who were charged with that task.

At the foot of the slope turn right onto the D50. After a short while you will pass the site of Aveluy Wood (Lancashire Dump) British Military cemetery on your left. This was started in June 1916 and was used by fighting units and Field Ambulances until the German retirement of February 1917. The original graves are scattered almost haphazardly at the foot of the slope to the left of the Great Cross. In September the graves of men killed in the area between the April and September of 1918 were dug in Plot 1, Row H. After the Armistice Plots II and III were added, nearer to the cemetery entrance gate, to accommodate isolated graves from within Aveluy Wood. In 1923 Rows I to M of Plot 1 were added by concentrations from a wider area. There are 360 graves within this cemetery of which 175 are unidentified.

Lancashire Dump lies above the Amiens - Albert - Arras railway line whose loss to the German advance had been so damaging to the British in the Arras - Albert area. At the southern end of the wood before the D50 road leaves the trees there are numerous trenches which are relatively accessible in good weather. All trenches in this vicinity were similarly named - Rig, Rag, Rope, Rut. Those on the eastern side of the railway and Ancre valley had a rather more imaginative sequence of names - Royalty, Ruling, Ribald and Rummage to name a few!

Across the low ground to the south Aveluy had become, during 1917, a very important junction in the British rail network. Between the southern end of Aveluy Wood and the military cemetery in Aveluy were a series of a dozen or more sidings and huge stores of materiel. The loss of this facility meant that the main rail route into this area was a single track running round the north of Mailly Maillet into Martinsart. The route of that single line can easily be seen on your IGN maps. From the site of the cemetery in Aveluy, or the D20 road towards Authuille, you can see the area whose flooding caused so many initial difficulties for the 38th Division's Welshmen who attacked here on 21st August during the preparatory operations prior to the opening of the Battle of Albert on 22nd August. The Welshmen's subsequent advance was to carry them across almost all of the 1916 battlefield, both north and south of the Albert - Bapaume road!

Walk Four.

The Longueval ridge area.

This walk covers the events surrounding the Welsh Division at Delville Wood as well as 122 Brigade RFA west of High Wood and the 18th Division at Trones Wood on 26/27th August. Again it has the advantage of a situation at the very heart of the 1916 battlefield and many fascinating sites from that era are within a mere stone's throw of this walk. This is a brief stroll lasting no more than one hour. Short detours would take you to High Wood and London cemetery as well as the complex of facilities and cemeteries within and close to Longueval.

Start at the cross roads within Longueval. Looking west takes your line of sight along the Longueval ridge which was attacked by 113 Brigade of the Welsh division on the morning of 26th August. Unfortunately that attack was unable to clear German machine gunners from the ridge and it was these men who subsequently caused so much damage to the 18th Division's advance across the north of Bernafay and Trones woods, just to the south of Longueval ridge. From the crossroads walk north towards the 1916 New Zealand memorial beyond the village. Past the houses the D197 forks off to the right in the direction of Flers and Bapaume. This is the location of 115 Brigade's advance across the north west of Delville Wood on 26th

Walk 4.

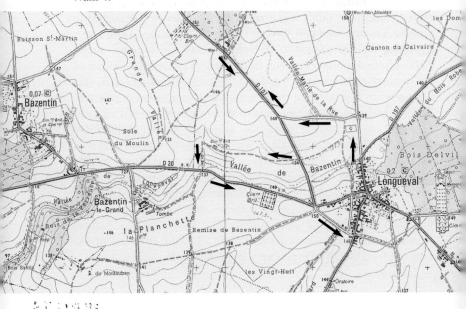

August. The following morning 114 Brigade moved through and eastwards to the D197. Walk a further 300 metres north and then turn left and walk for 700 metres until you strike the D107 which runs up past High Wood. From here you can look westwards across to Bazentin which the 38th Division had captured on the 25th. From here you can also visualise the extraordinary advance of 122 Brigade RFA across the Bazentin to High Wood road. Having got the guns across the plateau between Bazentin and High Wood 122 Brigade's men then engaged a German counter attack which was massing in the north of Delville Wood against 114 Brigade's men around the Flers road area.

Throughout that action 122 Brigade's guns were under severe enfilade machine gun fire from Longueval ridge and a 77mm battery within Longueval village. You can now walk along the rough track past Thistle Dump Cemetery towards the site of Caterpillar Valley cemetery on the high ground of Longueval ridge. Caterpillar Valley cemetery is a fascinating mixture of both 1918 and 1916. It contains an original and tiny cluster of 38th Division graves from the August of 1918 as well as a New Zealand memorial to the missing of September and October 1918. However, the bulk of the graves, concentrated here after the war, date from 1916.

From Caterpillar Valley cemetery walk back towards Longueval and turn right at the cross roads outside the village. Walk along the slightly sunken lane until you strike the Maricourt road, the D197. Cross the D197 and continue eastwards for a few yards. From the right hand or southern lip of the lane you can look out across the scene of the 18th Division's advance on 27th August during which the 8th Royal Berkshires, advancing from the direction of Montauban, were devastated by the German machine guns and rifles firing from the Longueval ridge and the location where you are now stood. This may be a good moment to refresh your memory of these events by looking again at Chapter 4.

From here it is a short walk back to your starting point at the central crossroads in Longueval. Continue eastwards and then turn left walking back into the village. As you strike the D20 road from Guillemont in Longueval you are where the German 77mm battery was in action opposing the guns of 122 Brigade RFA operating west of High Wood on this day, 27 August.

1. Because of the extensive nature of these tours it is impossible, within the confines of these pages, to produce an all embracing map. The IGN Serie Verte, sheet 4, Laon - Arras is sufficient for most of your needs in this context.
2. *London Gunners*. Kingham. Methuen & Co Ltd. 1919.
3. *Wilfred Owen*. Helen McPhail and Philip Guest. Leo Cooper/Pen & Sword, 1998.
4. Malard Wood is the western segment of the Bois de Celestins.
5. For cemetery details of this area see the Thiepval guide in this series.

181

INDEX

183

184